D1193729

Love, Infidelity, and Sexual Addiction

Love, Infidelity, and Sexual Addiction

A CODEPENDENT'S PERSPECTIVE

Christine A. Adams

Authors Choice Press

San Jose New York Lincoln Shanghai

Love, Infidelity, and Sexual Addiction
A Codependent's Perspective

All Rights Reserved © 2000 by Christine A. Adams

No part of this book may be reproduced or transmitted in any form or
by any means, graphic, electronic, or mechanical, including photocopying,
recording, taping, or by any information storage or retrieval system,
without the permission in writing from the publisher.

Authors Choice Press
an imprint of iUniverse.com, Inc.

For information address:
iUniverse.com, Inc.
5220 S 16th, Ste. 200
Lincoln, NE 68512
www.iuniverse.com

Originally published by Abbey Press

Copyright © 1992 by Christine A. McKenna

Cover Design by Scott Wannemuehler

The names and identifying details of the case histories,
and narrated portions, found in this book have been changed
Any resemblance to persons living or dead is coincidental.

ISBN: 0-595-15900-1

Printed in the United States of America

To Jennifer Schneider:
  —for her groundbreaking books
  —for her courageous example
  —for her words of encouragement
  —for her friendship

Contents

Introduction

The American public is not ready to talk seriously about sexual addiction. They either scoff at it or look on in disbelief. Another addiction? No one believes it except the sex addict and the coaddict who are living it. In an article in *USA Today* entitled "Sexual Addiction can Lead to Destruction," Marco R. della Cava opens by saying, "Sexual addiction is more apt to elicit snickers than concern. But addicts say it is no joke." And the persons living with the addicts agree.

Dr. Jennifer Schneider, M.D. in her second edition of *Sex, Lies and Forgiveness (1999)* states that "sexual addiction is a problem affecting perhaps 6 percent of Americans" or one out of every seventeen persons. Seventy percent of sexual addicts are also chemically dependent or suffering from other compulsive disorders. Additionally, 65 percent of females and 45 percent of addicted males have endured sexual abuse as children. Most sex addicts do not fit the stereotype of criminal offenders who satisfy their needs by forcing themselves on helpless victims. Some are prominent politicians, clergy, doctors, and other professionals.

The media capitalizes on any news story when prominent political and religious leaders fall from favor when their sexual behavior becomes compulsive. In the recent Clinton "sexgate" media frenzy, sexual addiction was often mentioned only as an after thought; or at best the people speaking with authority were ill informed.

On CNN, Mary Tillotson interviewed John Gray, the *Men Are From Mars, Women are from Venus* author, Ms. Ellen Fein, the *Rules* book's author, and Dr. Judy Kuriansky, a talk show/psychologist. The host asked about the possibility that Clinton might be afflicted with sexual addiction.

From the answers given, it was obvious that John Gray, a leading national speaker on couple communication therapy, was ignorant of the core issues of the addiction. Note that he blamed a lack of communication for Clinton's behavior. Could he mean that Hillary lacked communication skills? Ellen Fein made some innocuous statement about the marriage being wrong from the start because the woman didn't "play hard to get."

Dr. Kuriansky, with her medical background, spoke of the differing views on sexual addiction and stated three characteristics of the disease. She thought Clinton fit in two of the categories. Her information was at best incomplete, but at least headed in the right direction. The 1990's coverage of Clinton's seemingly compulsive sexual behaviors were moralistic, legalistic, or political, but rarely touched the issue of Clinton's real problem-his addiction.

The only coverage that seemed to ring true came from writers who are in recovery from the problem themselves, or prominent authorities working in the field. Douglas Weiss, family counselor and author, recently asked 2,000 recovering sex addicts who subscribe to his e-mail newsletter if they believe the president is an addict. Ninety-nine percent of those responding said, "Yes, he is one of us. If the allegations against the president are all true, you certainly have the classic picture of sexual addiction." Weiss himself simply said, "It looks like a duck and quacks like a duck." These are the comments of those who have lived through it.

In the 1930's, America began to deal with alcohol as an addiction. No longer did people say "if only he would control himself."

Some realized that the alcoholic is out of control or powerless over alcohol. Alcoholics Anonymous was formed and the Twelve Step Program created. In the 1970's society began to address drug addiction. In the 80's the medical profession studied addiction to food and gambling. Since the 1990's, we appear to be at the start of a serious movement looking at sexual addiction and its recovery.

Too often, sexual addiction has been cast as a moral problem. But with the interest in Bill Clinton's behaviors and Hillary Clinton's reactions, articles with a psychological or medical slant have cropped up. At the height of the presidential scandal, Lynette Clemetson and Pat Wingert in the Newsweek article "Clinton On the Couch" stated "Psychologists say Clinton's apparent problems are treatable-if he genuinely wants to solve them. The fumbling liaisons chronicled in the independent counsel's report, many therapists say, read like a checklist for sexual compulsion-self destructive risk-taking, and irrational justification, sex with less powerful sex partners. Even the details are mundane to those who treat this behavior. It is not uncommon for people with sexual compulsions to limit themselves to oral sex, experts say, or to stop before the point of climax. 'It enables them to feel less guilty,' says Dr. Gloria Harris, author of *Surviving Infidelity*."

When President Clinton showed he was willing to sacrifice his job, his wife, his daughter, the presidency and his country for sexual trysts with Monica Lewinsky, his behavior made no sense unless seen in the light of sexual addiction. Newsweek was forced to discuss difficult questions. Unintentionally, Bill Clinton may have opened the door to a closer look at this disease.

As the National Council on Sexual Addiction and Compulsivity states, "Addiction is a concept that traditionally was applied only to out of control use of alcohol and other drugs. Now, however, the term addiction is routinely used to describe behaviors such as gambling, overeating, and sex when they are out of control". "Sex addicts are able to sacrifice what they cherish most in order to preserve and continue their unhealthy behavior" says Patrick Carnes, who in 1993 wrote *Out Of The Shadows: Understanding Sexual Addiction*, the first and most basic text on the subject.

Dr. Jennifer Schneider M.D., Ph.D, medical director of Kachina Center for Addiction Recovery in Tucson, AZ, in an article entitled "How To Recognize Sexual Addiction" says,

"When sexual behavior is compulsive and continued despite serious adverse consequences, it is addiction. Sex addicts tend to sexualize other people and situations, finding sexual connotations in the most ordinary incident or remark. They spend great amounts of time and/or money in pursuit of a "quick fix." Any sexual behavior can be part of the addictive cycle: the context of the behavior must be considered to ascertain whether the behavior is compulsive. What is healthy sexual behavior for many people may be unhealthy for others, just as the use of alcohol causes no adverse consequences for most people but severe problems for some."

Dr. Schneider continues: "Sex addicts describe a euphoria with sex similar to that described by drug addicts with drug use. This may be an effect of endorphins and other endogenous brain chemicals, whereas the drug-induced state is externally produced. Like alcoholics and other drug addicts, sex addicts engage in distorted thinking, rationalizing, and defending and justifying their behavior while blaming others for resulting problems. They deny having a problem and make excuses for their behavior."

In 1992, the first printing of *Love, Infidelity and Sexual Addiction* was published under my maiden name, Christine A. McKenna. I explained the difference between normal sexual behavior and sexual behavior that is characterized by obsession and compulsion. Just as there is a distinction between the social drinker and the alcoholic, there is a distinction between the person who has an affair and the person who repeatedly has affairs even when they might lose their job, or marriage.

Also in this book, which was written from the codependent's perspective, I explained what I know best, the role of the coaddict caught in the throws of the cycle of their partner's addiction. Like Hillary Clinton, I was affected by a partner who was out of control. To survive, I needed to know about sexual addiction and coaddiction, I needed to change and recover from the repeated betrayals. Since 1992, I have found recovery and a new marriage where sexual addiction is not present. I am grateful to have come to this new place, and a new sense of self.

As Doug Weiss, in his book, *The Final Freedom*, says," we are in the early stages of understanding sexual addiction in our culture." The Clinton media frenzy with all its misinformation made that fact clear to me. I decided to reprint *Love, Infidelity and Sexual Addiction: From the Codependent's Perspective* in the hope that this book might continue to correct popular misconceptions, and bring new understanding and help to readers.

Love, Infidelity, and Sexual Addiction

ONE

Sexual Addiction

What is sexual addiction? It is a diseased state involving the sexual activities of the addict. It is a dysfunctional family or relational system that revolves around the sexual activities of the addict. It is a negative pattern of behavior that is compulsive, unmanageable, and continuous. Sexuality for some people causes destruction in their lives: it may mean disease, loss of job, conflict, shame, public censure, or suicide. When sexuality is causing that much trouble, it is out of control!

To further understand sexual addiction, it is necessary to understand the cycle it generates. Only then can patterns be recognized and the symptoms of the diseased state be recognized.

THE ADDICTIVE CYCLE

The first stage of the addictive cycle is sexual preoccupation. For the sex addict who has multiple affairs, it all begins with an intrusion into the thought processes. They see or meet someone who catches their attention. The meeting usually occurs in the same situation each time. For the teacher, it might be meeting a graduate student; for the doctor, a frightened patient; for the minister, a needy widow or confused divorcee. Usually, there is a pattern of contact before the stage of preoccupation.

Once the contact has been established, the addict needs to reconnect with the prospective lover. The addict arranges for more contact time. He or she becomes overly interested in assisting the

3

person or overly involved in a mutual project. Preoccupation increases as more and more time is spent preparing for contact with the prospective lover. Finally, the interruption of the thought processes leads to fantasy. Once sexual fantasy is entertained, it needs time for renewal and expansion. There will be extended periods of isolated thought at this stage. Perhaps the addict will stay up late at night, reading or watching TV. Generally, the addict will need more time alone than most people and will be agitated if he or she does not get it. Note, however, that a person who demands a great deal of space is not always an addict. In fact, there are times when that kind of behavior can indicate health. But if this symptom is a part of a larger pattern, there may be some need for concern.

As the addict's fantasy life intensifies, the addict will become more interested in the behaviors that surround the activity with the new love interest. For example, if the new lover does not show up as expected, the addict will be visibly affected. For someone who supposedly means so little, the interest level will be too high. Real disappointment will occur when a contact is not made.

In the second stage of the cycle of sexual addiction, the addict begins to practice certain ritualized behaviors. Ritualized behaviors are tried and true means of sexual procurement that all addicts practice: the looks, touches, and words they have found that always work with prospective lovers. Addicts who have multiple affairs have spent a lifetime perfecting those means of getting attention from others. It can be the way he or she makes eye contact, or the way a hand lingers on a shoulder or touches a special intimate place when giving a hug.

The behavior could be an exaggerated interest in the life of another or a kind of disdain, an aloofness that attracts some people. Whatever the behavior, it has been practiced before; it is ritualized. Subconsciously, the addict knows exactly what to do to assure procurement of loving attention. Certain rituals never fail!

For the most part, these examples refer to addictive behaviors of addicts who have affairs. There are many other behaviors that sex addicts become involved with: homosexual encounters, child molestation. All are different facets of the same disease, but all are cyclic, involving a carefully developed set of ritualized behaviors.

Patterns emerge around sexual behaviors. The sex addict goes to the same place, meets certain types of people, and gets into relationships by playing the same roles. They can be the helper, the spiritual leader, the psychiatrist, or just the gardener. But being available sexually is the message the addict projects.

As the cycle of addiction intensifies, the contact also intensifies. The "chase" is where the excitement is; it is the chase the addict revels in—whether it is in taking care of the crisis in the counselor's office or cruising the neighborhood. The chase is not confined to ordinary situations, for each addict has his or her own setups or triggers for the onset of compulsive ritualized behaviors.

Sex addicts do dangerous things. They get involved when they say they won't; they risk their jobs by having sexual relations with their clients.

When a person repeats negative behaviors which have negative consequences, they are out of control. Being out of control indicates compulsion. The ritualized behaviors that the addict gets involved in become a clear sign that they are into their addiction.

The third stage of the cycle of sexual addiction involves the actual compulsive behaviors—the acting out. It can be the meeting of the client and the doctor at some place other than the office where they can comfortably engage in sexual activity. It can be a one-night stand with a stranger. Ultimately, the sexual activity is always the final scene.

After the acting out, the fourth stage involves a sense of despair. It is like the morning after for the alcoholic. There is a terrible sense of remorse and shame. The addict asks, "Why did I do this?" A sense of powerlessness and impending doom is almost always felt.

In this final stage a sense of hopelessness sets in and the addict begins longing for contact with anyone: someone new, an old lover, a former spouse. There is that terrible empty feeling of being lost, alone, and incomplete. At this point, the cycle begins again with a chance meeting or a special look from someone. This creates a thought intrusion as someone reaches out to help the addict who find themselves in their hopeless state. The preoccupation begins and the cycle starts again.

CHARACTERISTICS OF THE ADDICT

At various times during this cycle, certain characteristics or symptoms become evident.

5

Denial

Sex addicts usually deny their addiction and look for reinforcement of their sexual promiscuity in friends or within society itself. It is not too difficult to find reinforcement because our society capitalizes on sex. The addict then denies his or her sexual behavior is causing life to become unmanageable. Just as an alcoholic seeks out other heavy drinkers, the sex addict sees love and sex in everybody. There is nothing that love will not cure.

Rationalization

To deny the existence of a problem, we need to rationalize away the problem. So it goes with sex addicts. They say, "I am not in trouble with my sexual behavior because I am a productive person. Of course, it is by compensation that I manage my job. I get up early to do extra work or I got to bed at 1:30 in the morning. I omit other things in life but I get my work done. I compensate so that I can meet Mary on Tuesday and Diane on Thursday, but I am at home with the kids and wife every weekend. If you ask me, I will tell you that my marriage is not affected by my affairs. In fact, my marriage is enhanced because my affairs bring warmth to my life." These are the rationalizations of addicts.

Sincere delusion

The symptom of delusion is characterized by the word *sincere* because it is just that. The addict sincerely believes his or her own lies. At the basis of all the negative, self-defeating behaviors lie these faulty core beliefs:

- I am basically a bad person.
- No one will love me as I am.
- My needs are never going to be met if I have to depend on others.
- Sex is my most important need.

These core beliefs delude the addict into faulty thinking. He or she sincerely believes these core truths, so why not act on them? The addict says, "If I am basically a bad person then I will have to lie to

6

cover my behavior. Since my needs will never by met by another, I will have to take care of my own sexual needs even if this means lying. No one can understand my needs anyway so I won't express them. I will have to lie to have my most important needs met. That is just a part of life!" Telling white lies is tantamount to sexual survival for the addict who sincerely believes that there is no other way.

Sometimes, in the guise of helping you or taking care of you, the sex addict exaggerates his or her importance to you. "If sex is my most important need, then perhaps it is yours." There can be abuse if the addict happens to be a member of a helping profession and the client happens to be needy.

Faulty core beliefs direct the addict into negative behaviors which he or she may see initially as a sincere desire to help others. However, when the cycle of addiction repeats itself, the addict feels remorse and shame, determining never to get into that situation again.

Like the alcoholic who repeatedly gets drunk, the sex addict swears off sex or takes a pledge "never to be unfaithful again." Yet, the core beliefs do not change, and when obsession and compulsion set in, the sexual acting out is repeated.

No one could deny the sincerity of the alcoholic as he or she comes off a disturbing drunk, promising to quit drinking. Usually, these promises get broken. So it is with the sex addict.

Paranoia

Because the cycle of addiction is so uncontrollable and the life of the addict so unmanageable, he or she lives in constant fear. That is the paranoia of this disease. How can they be sure their lies will not be revealed? How can they be sure they will not lose their family or their job? They can't. There is the ever-present fear of being found out.

So the addict lives in a panicked state, waiting for the ax to fall. However, the addict is not able to stop the terrible behaviors that cause the fears. Much like the alcoholic who fears the results of his drunken bouts, the addict apprehensively waits until the slip—the next drunk. The behavior is already out of control.

Blaming others

When you expect to be confronted, it is always good to have an excuse ready should someone accuse you. An excuse might be, "I wouldn't do this if I were not under such pressure," or "…if my wife were more loving," or "…if I really didn't like sex or need it." It can be a job or lack of one, a wife, husband, or lack of one, and so on. Blaming others is a symptom of sexual addiction. If the addict had to face self, he or she would have to admit the addiction and do something to correct it.

Like all addicts, sex addicts need their mind-altering substance—their sexual acting out—and they need to blame someone for it.

LEVELS OF THE DISEASE

The symptoms of this disease appear within the framework of the addictive cycle and at all levels of the disease. In *Out of the Shadows,* Patrick Carnes describes a workable structure which helps to identify behavior patterns that categorize sexual addiction in three levels. Refer to his chart on pp. 10-11.

> The first level, Level One, contains behaviors which are regarded as normal, acceptable, or tolerable. Examples include masturbation, homosexuality, and prostitution. Level Two, by contrast, extends to those behaviors which are clearly victimizing and for which legal sanctions are enforced. These are generally seen as nuisance offenses such as exhibitionism or voyeurism. The Level Three behaviors have grave consequences for the victims and legal consequences for the addicts such as incest, child molestation, and rape. Compulsivity at this level represents severe progression of the disease. (p. 57)

Level One addicts will not necessarily go to Level Three behaviors but escalation of the addiction is always a possibility. Addicts must understand their own pattern of sexually compulsive behavior. Subtle differences are extremely important, especially in early recovery. Once a pattern is identified, the cues or triggers and the rituals can be avoided.

It takes a competent therapist to determine the therapy the sex addict needs. It takes a strenuous, structured program of recovery with regular attendance at twelve-step group meetings.

Now there are twelve-step groups for sexual addicts and their families. They have different names: Sexaholics Anonymous, Sex and Love Addicts Anonymous, and Sexual Addicts Anonymous. They are not united at this time but are active all over this country and Europe. These groups function like the Alcoholics Anonymous Program.

It also takes a great deal of time, energy, and work to fight the addiction. Like alcoholism, this addiction is serious and insidious. It will destroy the persons who carry it as well as those who surround them. Many Level One addicts manage to remain unnoticed in society while Level Three addicts are imprisoned. All are addicts at different levels.

FAULTY CORE BELIEFS

As mentioned earlier, sex addicts operate with a set of negative core beliefs. These beliefs are usually generated within their family while they are growing up. Generally, they have low self-esteem and feelings of inadequacy.

The addict's first faulty belief is, "I am basically a bad person." The addict has learned from childhood that he or she deserves humiliation and feels unworthy. Yet, there is a show of self-importance, even grandiosity. But at the core of that delusional defense is the belief that he or she is bad. Children must be treated with disdain by adults in order to grow up feeling inadequate. The childhood of most addicts has distorted their self image, needs, and sexuality. Most Level Two and Level Three addicts have been sexually abused as children. Most Level One addicts have suffered some kind of covert emotional sexual abuse.

When the addict reaches adulthood, sexual compulsivity confirms the belief that he or she is unworthy. The addict hides the secret reality and presents the front of normalcy. The addict's entire family becomes sick as it centers around the addict's behavior. There is also evidence that sexual addiction moves from one generation to the next.

Society casts a special shame on sexual dysfunction and many people cast moral judgments upon any aberrant sexual behavior. The addict's sense of being unworthy is, therefore, confirmed in adult-

LEVELS OF ADDICTION

LEVEL OF ADDICTION	BEHAVIOR	CULTURAL STANDARDS
LEVEL ONE	Masturbation, heterosexual relationships, pornography, prostitution, and homsexuality	Depending on behavior, activities are seen as acceptable or tolerable. Some specific behaviors such as prostitution and homosexuality are sources of controversy.
LEVEL TWO	Exhibitionism, voyeurism, indecent phone calls, and indecent liberties	None of these behaviors is acceptable.
LEVEL THREE	Child molestation, incest, and rape	Each behavior represents a profound violation of cultural boundaries.

LEGAL CONSEQUENCES/ RISKS	VICTIM	PUBLIC OPINION OF ADDICTION
Sanctions against those behaviors, when illegal, are ineffectively and randomly enforced. Low priority for enforcement officials generates minimal risk for addict.	These behaviors are perceived as victimless crimes. However, victimization and exploitation are often components.	Public attitudes are characterized by ambivalence or dislike. For some behaviors such as prostitution there is a competing negative hero image of glamorous decadence.
Behaviors are regarded as nuisance offenses. Risk is involved since offenders, when observed, are actively prosecuted.	There is always a victim.	Addict is perceived as pathetic and sick but harmless. Often these behaviors are the objects of jokes which dismiss the pain of the addict.
Extreme legal consequences create high risk situations for the addict.	There is always a victim.	Public becomes outraged. Perpetrators are seen by many as subhuman and beyond help.

hood as the addiction is acted out.

The decisions and behaviors that surround sexual addiction are irrational and self-destructive. If you feel unworthy, then how can you make rational decisions? The whole family becomes shame-based. Unaware of their own pain, yet living in it, they operate under the sincere delusion that everything would be better if only the addict would change. Treating the entire family is critical because chances for recovery are greater once every member is fully aware of the disease.

Many times friends and family get angry at the addict's insensitivity to others as they witness inconsistency in word and action. In a pattern similar to the alcoholic, we believe the promise to stop only because we want to. We believe the addict will never be unfaithful again because he or she has promised not to be. For the co-addict who could make and keep such a promise, it seems rational. Unfortunately, because an addict is obsessive and compulsive, rational decisions are not always possible.

The second faulty core belief of an addict is, "No one will love me as I am." If I believe I am unlovable, then I cannot expect anyone to love me. If no one loves me, I can expect to be abandoned, to be alone. Nothing is permanent and I should not expect it to be so.

For the sex addict, there is a constant fear of abandonment, a constant search for love. It can produce a commanding aloneness, an acute sense of separateness. There is a fear of being dependent upon others, yet there is an insatiable need to be connected.

For the sex addict, there is no honest guilt or remorse. That would require honesty about the addiction. To stop the addiction would mean to stop the search for love. The thought of that is intolerable for the addict. As the disease of sexual addiction progresses, the addict feels more and more isolated.

A love and sex addict can be a master charmer, a manipulator and, generally, a lovable person. However, beneath that veneer is a core belief that he or she is unlovable. Why would anyone work so hard at being lovable if that person was not firmly convinced that he or she was not?

One of the charms of the addict is unattainableness. For some co-addicts that quality is desirable. Many times addicts make extravagant gestures of love in the midst of their unfaithfulness. This unpredictability can be very engaging for a coaddict whose parents were unpredictable.

It is important to note that the exterior view of the addict may not match interior core beliefs. One who believes he or she is unlovable will work hard to hide it.

The addict's third faulty core belief is, "My needs will not be met if I depend on others." If I don't expect my needs to be met, I will calculate, strategize, manipulate, and use others to get those needs met.

There is a basic deceptive stance in the lifestyle of the addict. It includes lies and secrets—then more lies and secrets!

Addicts feel a sense of rage and resentment because they have to manipulate others to be loved. It all goes back to the faulty beliefs: I am not worthy, I am not lovable, and I can't depend on anyone to meet my needs.

People need to be loved. It follows that whenever we anticipate rejection we will react. The last thing the addict does is to express his or her needs to others. On the surface it would seem that the addict does not need or want anything. Yet under that facade is the deceit—the manipulation of trying to be affirmed and cared for without expressing the need. The addict may choose the kind of profession that allows him or her to "collect" needy people. The addict might be a counselor, teacher, minister. However, no matter what the aura of respect or the role played, there will be inconsistencies in the addict's public and private life if sexual addiction exists.

The fourth and final faulty core belief of the sex addict is "Sex is my most important need." Addicts confuse sex with nurturing and caring. Since they are so in need of nurturing and caring, sex becomes the addict's most important need. It becomes a shallow and empty activity that provides a means of affirmation.

If I am unworthy, if I feel others will not meet my needs, if no one loves me as I am, then I will try to disprove those core beliefs through physical contact with others. In a society that sexualizes almost everything, it is easy to confuse nurturing and sex.

The addict experiences a certain terror in thinking of life without sex. Even though the sex activity never meets the needs of the addict, he or she spends a great deal of time trying to structure situations to guarantee the availability of a sexual partner.

Because sexual obsession pervades the life-style of the addict, he or she fears a loss of control. Like the alcoholic who is always trying to stop drinking, the sex addict is always trying to stop or limit sexual activity.

Like the alcoholic who keeps bottles hidden in a closet, the sex addict also keeps a supply of resources: sex partners everywhere. Intimate relationships are never ended, but are kept open in case they're needed later.

Sexual addiction represents a pathological relationship where sexual obsession replaces people. Sexuality is surrounded with negative rules, judgments, and messages about sex. Sex is the most important need for the addict.

Perhaps in the family of origin it was intimated that being sexual was being perverse. Perhaps the only source of comfort for the child was secret sexual activity. Thus, sex became a response to pain and loneliness.

Victims of sexual abuse often become sex addicts at one level or another. They may be the victims themselves or they may have grown up in the presence of sexual abuse. Treatment is important because the personal history of sexual compulsion within each family plays an important part in the development of the addiction.

Although sexual addiction is like alcoholism, recovery from sexual addiction is comparable to recovery from compulsive overeating. A food addict has to learn to eat normally and a sex addict has to learn to be a sexual person in a healthier way. The sex addict learns to focus, not on the sex act itself, but on all that precedes it: those feelings that accompany initial contact with a new lover; winning the lover over with sensitivity, openness, and attention; and finally, the sex act itself. The coaddict married to the addict is in a no-win situation because the coaddict can never provide what it is that intrigues his or her partner most—the conquest of a new lover.

Recovery for the addict means giving up the chase! It takes a qualified counselor to help the addict monitor his or her own behavior. But the first step for the addict is to recognize the problem and to ask for help. More and more people are doing just that.

And that is the good news of this book. There is hope for the sex addict. Twelve-step groups, organized across the country, meet regularly. With the help of such groups, thousands of addicts are getting immediate support. Several medical centers provide inpatient treatment for sex addicts. There is little understanding among the general public but as time passes, more and more resources for help spring up. There is hope and there is recovery from this addiction.

CHAPTER

TWO

Sexual Coaddiction

Sexual coaddiction occurs in conjunction with sexual addiction. It occurs because the partner of the sex addict has a set of negative core beliefs similar to that of the addict. It occurs because the co-addict willingly enters into the addictive cycle *with* the addict. There are discernible symptoms and characteristics of this sickness. They include denial, obsession, compulsive behavior, loss of self-esteem, and isolation from others. Ironically, the very love that is sought eludes the coaddict as he or she is caught up in addiction to the addict.

There is something about the betrayal aspect of sexual addiction that defies the written word. It is not the initial betrayal; it is the moment when you realize you have been betrayed again.

The pain seems to intensify with each betrayal until you can't stand it any longer. I can remember the first time I realized that the wonderful, beautiful love affair I had been experiencing was a sham. I could have died from the grief of it—I felt everything I treasured was dirty, sordid, and cheap. I got over it and readjusted my perceptions—right back into the addiction.

Then the second betrayal came. It seemed worse than the first, a far more grievous, personal slight which cut deeper and deeper into me. The anger was more intense, the trust was shattered, and forgiveness was not readily available. Then came the final betrayal which cut the deepest of all.

Finally, through the pain, I realized that my husband had to be very sick to hurt so many women repeatedly. We couldn't be real to

15

him if he did not realize the pain he was inflicting—or we were allowing him to inflict on us.

The pain was staggering because it never seemed to stop. It just intensified with each blow. Yet, all the women involved seemed willing to step up for more and more abusive treatment. I realized the extent of my own sickness when I realized that each one of us had asked to be betrayed again. We were so willing to pay the price for staying in our addiction. We cooperated. We were coaddicts.

THE COADDICTIVE CYCLE

Any cycle of addiction is a no-win situation as it starts in denial and leads to despair and remorse. The remorse triggers the addiction and the futile cycle of denial starts again.

Coaddicts are often codependent persons whose core identity is not developed or is unknown. They maintain a false identity built from dependent attachments to external sources: partners, spouses, families, appearances, work, or the roles they play. They create an illusion of self from which to operate.

The coaddict gains his or her identity from the addict. Therefore, the coaddict, too, is caught up in the cyclic behaviors of the addict. The coaddict does not revolve on his or her own but is propelled by this outside force. Until the coaddict disengages the destructive rolling motion of this diseased state, it will go on and on, gaining momentum. Like a ball rolling downhill, it will gain speed as it descends. The addictive process is self-perpetuating and progressive.

Unfortunately, until the coaddict becomes disengaged from the addict, whether inside or outside the relationship, the cycle of dysfunction will continue. This cycle has six steps.

The preoccupation

Just as the addict is preoccupied with his or her sexual encounters, the coaddict is preoccupied with the sexual activities of the addict. Early in the relationship, the coaddict makes a conscious effort to be uncontrolling and may even avoid setting limits in order to give the addict the impression that he or she is not controlling. But the coaddict will eventually notice that the lover is inordinately interested in others and in sex. Obsessive and compulsive behaviors are always apparent. Given time, the coaddict will notice the behaviors.

The denial

At first, the coaddict denies the partner's infidelities. The coaddict says, "I am imagining the whole thing," or "I am just being jealous," or "I shouldn't let such things bother me." The coaddict rationalizes the addict's behavior but blames the addict at the same time.

Ritualized behaviors

After the initial denial, the coaddict begins to act compulsively through ritualized behaviors. The coaddict becomes hypervigilant, watching to see if there are others in the addict's life or if it is just imagination. The coaddict starts to control behaviors to gain assurance of the addict's undivided attention. The coaddict resorts to ritualized compulsive behaviors such as frantically checking up on the lover or always being there so no one else will be. The coaddict tries to assure the fidelity of the addict.

Acting out—the demand for love

The addict responds to the coaddict's ritualized behaviors by moving farther and farther away, entering his or her own ritualized compulsive behavior. The addict begins to wander. The coaddict becomes even more controlling and ritualized and finally demands the addict's love. The addict senses and resists the controls and becomes even more compulsive. At this point the addict feels driven to act out sexually. The coaddict delivers an ultimatum.

Loss of self

The coaddict's demand for love is rejected. Since the addict is the coaddict's whole identity, the coaddict feels a loss of self. Oftentimes, the coaddict finds out about the lover or lovers and the relationship is broken.

Despair and remorse

The coaddict feels a sense of isolation as the despair and remorse deepen. Similarly, the addict, having acted out, feels a sense of guilt and despair. The addict also feels isolated and may make a frantic attempt to move back toward the coaddict. For awhile, the coaddict may focus on self. Eventually, however, the coaddict may once again become preoccupied with the addict, and the cycle is on again.

The charts on pages 20-21 explain more clearly how the behaviors of the addict and the coaddict interweave within the cycle of addiction.

CORE BELIEFS

Coaddiction happens because the coaddict holds on to certain erroneous beliefs. No matter what others tell the coaddict, these beliefs seem viable and true. They register within the very core of the person, subconsciously recorded; therefore, they are acted upon as if viable and true.

These erroneous core beliefs come from the codependent's family of origin. The coaddict often comes from a dysfunctional family that was incapable of affirming the coaddict or setting him/her on a positive path. Parents are evaluated by their ability to impart positive messages to their children. These positive messages should touch on love, security, acceptance, discipline, guidance, independence, protection, and faith. Parents who may have learned negative messages from their own parents cannot be blamed entirely. However, they contribute to these negative views.

Many coaddicts are ACOAs—children brought up in families that addiction controls; brought up in families where children's needs were not met; brought up in families where children heard negative messages in the early developmental stages of childhood. This is where many coaddicts learned what they still believe.

To have a positive self-image, children need to hear positive messages: You are lovable, you are safe, you are OK, you are in control, you will be helped, you are mature, you are protected, you can have faith in God. In the dysfunctional home, however, children hear negative messages: You are not lovable, you are not safe, you are not OK, you are not mature, you are not protected, you cannot have faith in God.

It is these negative messages that the adult child brings to primary relationships. Hearing negative messages makes a child doubt his or her self-worth. The child knows something is terribly wrong and begins to have self-doubts. When it is time to couple, the adult brings these doubts and core beliefs to the relationship.

FAULTY CORE BELIEFS

The coaddict's first faulty core belief is, "I am not a worthwhile person and no one will ever love me as I am." It's understandable that if you do not value yourself, you will seek to have others value you in a demanding, addictive way. If you believe you are not worthwhile, it makes sense that you will seek those who do not value themselves or their love.

However, if you do not feel lovable, you will seek someone who seems to be very loving and accepting of others but, in truth, is unavailable—someone like a sexually addicted person.

In the coaddict's faulty belief system is a basic distrust of the other's love. The coaddict is not generally open to being loved, of accepting love as a given. Consequently, the coaddict appears to be needy and hesitant.

This hesitancy may be covered up with a superficial exterior. Generally, the coaddict gives the appearance of being self-sufficient. He or she seems unaffected by problems and often conceals problems so no one will see the pain.

Coaddicts have a tendency to take on extra responsibility by trying to be all things to all people, especially the addict. Why would anyone assume the responsibility for another's sexual behavior? The coaddict believes he or she has the power to control that person. This is a basic egocentric assumption of the coaddict.

What makes the coaddict think he or she has that power to control others? Perhaps the coaddict tries to dominate or overnurture in a relationship in order to be intimate without risk. Perhaps the idea of separation is so frightening that the coaddict would sacrifice anything not to lose the love of the addict.

Whatever it is that prompts the coaddict, there is a self-righteousness and a grandiosity that masks the real issues. It is this attitude the addict uses to advantage.

The coaddict protects family secrets even when this enables the addict to "stay sick." The coaddict does this in the name of love, marriage, children, or career. Something within causes the coaddict to assume responsibility for another's actions. That is coaddiction!

Patrick Carnes writes the following:

Co-addicts operate with the belief, *I am basically a bad, unworthy person.* Because they share this belief with the addicts, they par-

Addictive Cycle: Coaddict

PREOCCUPATION	Notices addict's preoccupation with others, has exaggerated love interest in addict.
DENIAL	Rationalizes behavior, blames addict, says "This is not happening to me."
RITUALIZED BEHAVIORS	Obsession—compulsive rituals of control and hypervigilance—sets in. Notices addict's behavior; more controls are used.
ACTING OUT	Demands love. Delivers an ultimatum and is rejected.
LOSS OF SELF	Disconnected, no communication, isolation.
DESPAIR AND REMORSE	Feels alone and abandoned.
RETURNS TO SELF	Returns to self and known activities and friends.
HONEYMOON PERIOD	Relationship gets better.

Cycle starts again

Signs of Recovery in Coaddict

1. Focus on self
2. Acceptance of codependency in self
3. Not blaming addict
4. Changed behaviors to stop cycle
5. Detaching with no *demands* for love
6. Personal respect and dignity maintained
7. No despair, remorse
8. New interests
9. A happier person
10. New freedom

Addictive Cycle: Addict

PREOCCUPATION	Addict preoccupied with others, notices coaddict's interest and resists.
DENIAL	Rationalizes behavior, blames coaddict, says "This is not happening to me."
RITUALIZED BEHAVIORS	Obsession with prospective lover—compulsive rituals of control and hypervigilance set in. Notices coaddict's controls; resists more.
ACTING OUT	Acts out sexually with partner other than spouse.
LOSS OF SELF	Disconnected, no communication, isolation.
DESPAIR AND REMORSE	Feels alone and abandoned.
RETURNS TO COADDICT	Returns to an interest in coaddict.
HONEYMOON PERIOD	Relationship gets better.

Cycle starts again

Signs of Recovery in Addict

1. Focus on self-recovery program for sexual addiction
2. Acceptance of addiction
3. Not blaming coaddict
4. Changed behaviors—avoiding circumstances that cause "slips"
5. Detaching from other sexual situations
6. Personal respect and dignity maintained
7. No despair, remorse
8. New interests
9. A happier person
10. New freedom

ticipate in the addictive system easily. Co-addicts grow up in families in which their self-worth is constantly in jeopardy. Feelings of inadequacy and failure parallel the addicts' sense of unworthiness. Not believing there are any options, co-addicts tolerate abusive, humiliating, and degrading behavior. Being with an addict furthers the myth of "unlovability."

Self-righteous disdain often masks the interior fears of the co-addict. Also, aggressive and critical controlling behavior switches with compliant enabling roles. Co-addicts report that these switches can occur within moments of each other. Either position shares a martyrdom in which the co-addict is being "victimized." (*Out of the Shadows*, p. 102)

The second faulty core belief of the coaddict is, "If I'm not a worthwhile person, then I will have to pay for love." The addict values sex as his or her most important need and will bargain and trade anything for it. It is no wonder that the addict and the coaddict get together. One is looking for a way to buy love and approval and the other is looking for love and approval through sexual activity.

This behavior stems from the belief that love has a price tag. The coaddict believes that caretaking and sex are the price for being loved. For the coaddict, sex becomes the payment for love.

An addictive relationship includes a kind of 'all or nothing' thinking. If sex represents love, then the absence of it can be threatening. Sex addicts have great control over coaddicts because they control the most important sign of love. For coaddicts suffering from low self-esteem and the feeling of being unworthy, taking away love can cause severe identity problems.

The identity of most codependents comes from outside. Because they have so little individuation, coaddicts give anything for outside approval. The tragedy of the coaddictive situation is that coaddicts do not feel they have the 'rights' that others do. They assume that situations which lack boundaries are normal. But this is not so. All situations have certain parameters that must be observed.

The coaddict feels obligated to submit to unacceptable sexual situations, often participating sexually when he or she does not desire to. Prompting these actions is the fear that if you do not do what I ask, then I will find another who will and I will leave you. This is threatening, especially for someone who doubts he or she is worthy of the love of another.

People in addictive relationships tend to keep score. They practice conditional love. If you do something for me, I will do something for you. The idea of unconditional love is absent.

An active addict whose most important need is love will convey the message that sexual acts will assure you favor. In addition to providing sexual activity, the coaddict will often be especially caring toward the addict. The coaddict will try to please the partner in all ways—often to personal detriment.

The third negative core belief of the coaddict is, "My needs are never going to be met if I depend on someone else." As children, we develop a perception of the world and our relationship to it. We estimate our relationship to parents and other family members. If our experience of these relationships always proves that our needs will not be met, then we grow up assuming this will be the case in adult life as well. Many times it is the only reality we have ever known.

For example, the adult child of an alcoholic (ACA) has many needs that were not met. The ACA who marries an addicted person will continnue to have neglected needs. Neglect is the only reality the ACA has ever known. Consequently, the coaddict assumes his or her needs are less important and must be put on hold while the addict's are met. Ultimately, the coaddict learns that he or she alone must take care of personal needs if they are to be met at all.

No one can live with long-term neglect. Having needs met is essential to our survival as human beings. A person who is emotionally neglected, unnurtured, or physically abused will eventually wither and die.

What is most tragic about our situation as coaddicts is that we allow it. The self-condemnation fostered by such a situation is debilitating. No one can be neglected for long without becoming frustrated, angry, and disturbed. We become less lovable, and when this happens our lovers abandon us. Our core beliefs come true.

The coaddict's fourth negative core belief is, "I will be abandoned." This is a self-fulfilling prophecy, a no-win situation. When persons are not nurtured, they lose hope and become unattractive to others. Their partners tire of the hopeless attitude and leave.

Finding themselves alone, many coaddicts quickly enter another relationship equally as addictive. The old pattern emerges and the ultimate abandonment happens again. The ending of a second relationship is disconcerting because it confirms what the coaddict knew

23

all along: he or she is not worthwhile, there is a price to pay for love, needs will not be met, and he or she will be abandoned. The cycle goes on and the coaddict is again the victim of these negative core beliefs.

Positive people do not believe they are worthless. They believe they are children of God with great value. They do not believe caretaking and sexual favors comprise love, nor do they believe their needs will not be met. Because they reach within to satisfy their needs, and to others outside themselves, they become accustomed to being satisfied rather than dissatisfied. Healthy people know and understand they can and will be loved for a long time in a healthy relationship. They realize that they can win at love because they are already doing so.

For the sex addict obsessed with chasing romance, there is no love. For the coaddict obsessed with chasing the addict, there is no love.

Why? Because the coaddict and the addict accept their negative core beliefs as internalized convictions. They are under a sincere delusion. They do not know that they do not know.

Love is patient and kind, not boastful, arrogant, or rude. It does not seek its own way. It is quiet and gentle. Addictive love is chaotic, tumultuous, noisy, and rough.

CHARACTERISTICS OF SEXUAL COADDICTION

Being the victim

A key characteristic of sexual coaddiction is the constant attitude of being a victim. Sometimes being a victim is so inbred that the coaddict assumes he or she must remain so. Being a victim can mean being controlled by the sexual demands of the addict since the addict gives the message to comply or be betrayed. This message is so powerful that the coaddict will do almost anything to keep the relationship open and viable.

Nothing is more enabling to the behavior of an addict than to have a person willing to keep the relationship open at all cost. Someone who sets limits and boundaries is not a desirable partner to the addict; the addict will seek out a lover who does not set limits.

The addict needs many such coaddicts to supply sex, romance, or love. But the coaddicted partner who chooses to stay in that role as victim is a willing victim.

24

* * *

It was twenty-four hours before the court date and I was still belaboring my decision. My husband wanted a divorce to marry someone else, but I wanted to hang on. My husband was a sex addict and I knew there was adequate proof to substantiate this. But what if he had gone to treatment? What if I had gone to more programs? Couldn't I have handled it differently? I didn't know.

Then my mind drifted back to all the infidelities. I listened to myself as these words reverberated within: ...*what he did to me*.

Suddenly I realized I was playing the victim. The role had been thrust upon me, but I accepted it. What could I do to turn this around? Then it occurred to me that I might simply step out of the victim role. *Just do it! Act, don't react.*

That night I picked up the phone and called my husband. In a conversation, neither punitive nor damning but firm and inflexible, I told him I wanted the divorce. It was my choice. I would no longer play the role of victim. Somehow I knew that the decision would eventually make me free. I had to know that I was no longer a victim.

* * *

Not all victims have to reach the divorce stage before stepping out of the victim role. Victims must understand that separating from the addict does not solve the problem. The problem is to remain out of that victim role.

Many couples find recovery together if they get help. It is possible to stay in a relationship and still step out of the victim role. For years, partners of alcoholics have accomplished this through AlAnon. Partners of sex addicts who are diligent in their work in SAnon have been successful also. Trying to go it alone is almost impossible and can lead to these damaging results:

- The coaddict loses his or her sense of identity
- The coaddict becomes powerless over his or her own life.
- Harmful consequences occur.

Loss of identity occurs when the coaddict turns over his or her identity to the addict. This causes great personal instability.

When persons reach outside of themselves to become whole, they are on dangerous ground. What if that source runs dry? What if that

25

source is not available? What if the source is incapable of making the person whole? Such persons risk their ability to function alone.

Coaddicts are willing victims. They turn themselves over to lovers with an abandon that is frightening. The abandon goes beyond risk and daring; it touches on a lack of prudence and wisdom. Coaddicts are so sure that being connected to another will make them whole that they willingly give themselves away.

The second damaging result of being a victim is that the coaddict becomes *powerless over his or her life*. This is a paradox; the co-addict seems to be so controlling when, in reality, the addict is in complete control.

The panic of victims is so palpable that they will do almost anything to end it. But because victims are reactors, not actors, they believe themselves powerless to change the situation. They convince themselves that the addict has all the control. Victims give up their identities to another and are powerless over their own lives. They are addicted to the addict.

In her book, *Women, Sex and Addiction* (New York: Harper & Row Publishers, Inc., 1989, p. 3), Charlotte Davis Kasl describes the codependent woman as a victim of life who takes her cues from the outside world; a victim who believes that if she lets go of the security of external forms like house, husband, or status she "will fall into a terrifying emptiness. She fears she could not exist on her own." Kasl describes the codependent woman as a child "who has not left the mother's arms, so she clings to forms, to people and things representing security as if they were life itself." Indeed, she is a woman who feels powerless.

Feeling powerless. Feeling like a victim. Feeling unable to act. These are terrible feelings. The only escape is to step out of the victim role.

The final result of remaining in the victim role is that it may cause *harmful consequences*. A person who feels controlled and in constant danger feels fear.

Being out of control for long periods of time causes anxiety and tension. Sometimes coaddicts become fueled by this tension and get a "high" from crisis. For an ACA, it might be the only way they have ever lived. This anxiety and tension can be used to gain a sense of control.

But long periods of intensity are not the same as long periods of intimacy. Burnout follows intensity. With burnout, there could be depression. No one can sustain these highs and lows without a fall.

Due to the constant fear of betrayal, the anxiety of my own compulsive behavior, and the tension my husband's affairs caused, I felt really sick. My life had an edge that never went away. I could feel the pain of that edge everywhere I went. It encompassed my whole mind and body. The only relief I ever got was when I prayed.

* * *

There is a general sadness that follows as the coaddict acts out his or her part of the addiction. The addict who is actually betraying the coaddict appears charming and popular; the coaddict appears lost and sad. When the coaddict pulls away from friends and others in social settings, they welcome it. Consequently, the truth of the coaddict's situational sadness may never be revealed.

To escape, the coaddict may enter into other addictions such as food, work, or spending. It is only logical that other addictions might cover a primary one. Often the coaddict will seek sobriety from alcoholism only to find this relational addiction in place. Harmful consequences come from all addictions. One addiction may sometimes lead to another. When this is the case, there is much work to be done. It is necessary to have competent counseling to unravel the interplay of addictions. If several addictions are involved, the sexual addiction may not be addressed for years.

In any addictive relationship is a failure to develop God-given talents. There is a loss of time and energy to the addiction. When the husband cheats and the wife engages in hypervigilance, both are expending time and energy on something other than themselves or their relationship. Their own spiritual growth and their loving relationship is being lost. These losses are the harmful consequences of a coaddict who plays the victim and an addict who is active. Ultimately, love and life become unmanageable.

The unmanageable life

Life becomes unmanageable for the coaddict as the cycle of addiction goes on. If recovery does not take place, the situation worsens. An environment that fosters tension, depression, and fear often produces baleful consequences. Many coaddicts are moved to action when they feel their life slipping away.

One consequence of coaddiction is physical sickness which occurs when the coaddict tries to deal with the anxiety, depression, and fear. Coaddiction is not a reality-based situation. Thinking is impaired and true feelings are not expressed. As a result, serious physical sickness such as stomach ulcers or frequent bouts of flu can occur. Whatever form it takes, physical sickness can mask mental and emotional problems. In addition, sickness can cause loss of work, money, and sometimes missed career opportunities.

Accidents are another consequence of coaddiction. The coaddict is often tired, sick, or distracted and may invite accidents while driving or in the home. Even more disconcerting is that the children of coaddicts are often the victims. Accidents cause more confusion, more crises, and more loss. As the losses escalate, the coaddict becomes more anxious and depressed.

Coaddiction can produce severe depression—a serious condition that may require hospitalization. Many persons with severe depression attempt suicide. This is the ultimate sign of an inability to manage life. It stands to reason that extended years of anxiety and fear might cause a person to lose sight of all that is positive and hopeful in life.

Unfortunately, it may take some years for the coaddict to "bottom out." This is because most coaddicts have a tremendous tolerance for suffering. Being a victim feels natural and comfortable; it may be all the coaddict has ever known.

Hitting bottom can take place within the relationship or after it has ended. When it happens doesn't really matter. The addiction is the problem, not the sex addict or his/her actions.

An event that triggers a reversal or a conversion may be simple or quite shocking. For example, an arrest for sexual exhibitionism or another final affair may throw the coaddict into a period of withdrawal.

Withdrawal or disengagement

There is a pattern of withdrawal in recovery from coaddiction just as there is a pattern of progression into the diseased state.

An immense sense of abandonment and a terrible sense of remorse are early signs of withdrawal. These are symptoms that sex addicts experience as well. Many times both partners hit this point at the same time and the relationship breaks apart.

It takes a great deal of outside help for both partners to get through this period. Commitment to the marriage, love of the spouse, or concern for the children of the union won't necessarily insure permanence. If addiction is wreaking havoc on the relationship, it will have to be rebuilt. That takes guidance and work.

The key is to seek knowledgeable assistance as soon as possible. The right kind of help is important. To deal with a psychotherapist who has no knowledge of sexual addiction and coaddiction is useless.

A legal separation or divorce often ends an addictive relationship. It seems the final act, intended to bring relief to a horribly painful situation. However, it is often precipitous. Many times separation or divorce does not end the addictive behavior. Until all the puzzle pieces have been put together, until all loose ends have been tied, a separation or divorce won't be the final separation for the lovers. If the addict has left for another coaddict, it could appear to be the end. Yet, the rejected coaddict may hang on, hoping for a reconciliation, staying in the addiction and experiencing continued pain.

* * *

Mary, a lovely thirty-five-year-old business executive, came to SAnon with her incredible story. After months of alienation from her addict husband, now returned to his former wife, Mary made plans to divorce him. It was not what she wanted to do but what she needed to do to save her own dignity and peace of mind.

On the day of the court appearance she called her husband. He seemed defensive and arrogant. She learned he already had plans for his third marriage, a remarriage to his first wife. Nevertheless, Mary told him she loved him and had always hoped for reconciliation. She spoke about the pain she felt during the separation.

To indicate her forgiveness, she said she believed their reconciliation had already taken place in the mind and heart of God and that she was at peace with herself. He accepted this and they prayed together that she would have the courage to do what needed to be done the next day.

The next day Mary divorced her husband. That afternoon he called her, but she told him she was too upset to talk. There was a pause on the other end of the line. Finally he said, "I have never loved anyone the way I love you. I still love you and will always love you."

They discussed what went wrong in the relationship and what they might have done to stop the estrangement. He acknowledged the final good-bye letter she had mailed. She spoke of her struggle of wanting to be with him physically. He said he wanted to be with her at that moment. When he hung up he said "good-bye for now." A week later he remarried his first wife.

This is the language of sexual addiction. This demonstrates the co-addict hanging on and the addict protecting a possible supply. The pattern is so predictable; it is likely the addict had kept his former wife strung out on expectations when he married Mary.

An objective outsider might look at this situation and say the man is insane to remarry his first wife when he claims to love his second. However, from the standpoint of addiction—a standpoint which omits the possibility of genuine love—this story makes sense.

How can an addict keep so many willing partners so long? There is a carefully mastered set of love expressions administered to the proper people at the proper time.

On the day Mary's ex-husband married his former wife, he cried openly in joy of this reunion. He really believed his own tears. He really believed his own profession of love and fidelity to his former wife. She believed that the man she was marrying had never loved his second wife, that he had made a terrible mistake when he married Mary. The cycle of sexual addiction had started again. Within a month Mary heard from her ex-husband again.

At the time of withdrawal, it is important to consider the following: *timing, the need for structure, slips, transference of feelings,* and *the need to find self.*

Timing. Everything has a place and time—so it is in an early recovery. Withdrawal from any addiction is a critical and treacherous period. Like alcoholics in early recovery, codependents can easily return to the unhealthy relationship that they left or get involved in new situations that are dangerous.

I remember being amazed that time passed so quickly when I left my addict partner. I felt freed of this terrible weight and could now move unencumbered. However, when the reality of my situation set in and I started to experience the pain of being alone, time slowed to a deadly pace and hung heavy on my hands.

Recovery from any addiction involves a definite process. The recovering person needs to accept the timing of recovery. If not, he or she might become stuck in one of the stages of the process. There is a time to feel feelings, rethink thoughts, and get well. Although they can be laboriously painful, changes mean growth.

The early recovery period is a good time to say, "I am not ready for that yet," or "It is not a good time for me today, this week, this year."

The need for structure. There is a paradox here. The recovering person needs to be free to make decisions about those things which take up time; yet there is an undeniable need for structure as well.

A schedule of activities can help fill time. Nothing is more devastating than being alone; nevertheless, if a person doesn't spend sufficient time alone, healing will not take place. A delicate balance is necessary.

At this critical time one needs to find the proper structure to enhance life. It may be SAnon meetings which help the families of sex addicts, or a spiritual program at church. This is the time to seek the community's help. Good friends and relatives are needed to carry the recovering person through this time of transition.

An active work schedule is also good. It isn't wise to shift or quit jobs. Change what is necessary but keep familiar structural supports in place.

A break in an addictive relationship can mean that one's world is swept away. A person married to a dominating person may experience a tremendous shift in emphasis and activities. Perhaps a whole new support system will have to be developed.

Slips. For the codependent person, the process of recovery is not always a steady, positive progression. There are setbacks. Slips involve falling back into negative behaviors.

Slips can be physical. Perhaps sexual guidelines established with the addict are broken or a period of sexual abstinence is not maintained. These are slips.

Slips can be emotional. The coaddict may return to the obsession of the addiction. He or she may deny, rationalize, or return to ritualized compulsive behaviors. Recovery does not happen immediately nor will it ever be perfect. It took years to create the codependent state; it will take years to generate an independence worthy of a child of God.

Asking God for help along the way is extremely important. When

31

people lose faith and seem to slip backward, they need to maintain hope and courage. They need a source of power greater than themselves if they are to succeed.

The transference of feelings. At the time of withdrawal, feelings come from all directions. The coaddict can feel sad, cheated, angry, and relieved—all at the same time.

It is important to identify a feeling and understand why it is happening. Without this step, negative feelings get transferred to others. Innocent family members bear the brunt of withdrawal unless emotions are expended in an appropriate manner.

When there is loss, there is emotional reaction. When there is addiction, there is loss.

The need to find self. The most devastating loss in the addictive process is the loss of self. During recovery the lost identity needs to be found.

Impaired thinking makes the coaddict blind to personal separateness. The coaddict really believes that not being loved by one's lover makes one unlovable. Having concentrated on controlling love so long, he or she has no self—no identity— without it.

After much struggle as a coaddict, I finally came to understand that the problem to address was me. I could have gone on for years checking and rechecking the addict without ever looking at my own role in the addiction. I could have continued directing his show and never looked at mine.

In the book, *A Course in Miracles* (Tiburon, California: Foundation for Inner Peace, 1976), is this wise observation: "You think you hold against your brother what he has done to you. But what you really blame him for is what you did to him."

I have come to know this truth in dealing with my coaddiction. What I did was to hold him too tightly so that he could not grow, to need him too much, to put him before God and all others, to crush his spirit. What I did was to try to keep him from his own sins so that those sins would not hurt me.

Ultimately, I held him back from pain, growth, and spiritual awareness. I allowed him to be dependent on me when, in reality, I was dependent upon him. The truth, however, is that we are both separate and dependent on God. We had rejected God and made gods of each other. We did not love in a spiritual sense, but only in a physical sense—and it was never enough. So we lost it all. We lost ourselves.

In the withdrawal period is a moment of breaking free—a time when the denial is broken, the obsession lifts, and an actual disengagement from the lover begins. It comes when the coaddict realizes that he or she is lovable even if a lover does not choose to love in return.

Ken Keyes' book, *How to Make Your Life Work* (Coos Bay, Oregon: Love Line Publications, 1974), changed my thinking. Keyes speaks of "addictive demands" and "preferences." These concepts made me realize that I had been addictively demanding that my husband love me, hoping he would change his mind and love me again. It was making me terribly unhappy. In analyzing my addictive demand, I asked myself some core questions. Why was it so important that he love me? Why not someone else? Then I realized I had convinced myself that without his love I would be unlovable.

The impact of this realization struck me. In his addiction, the addict could not love me. Yet I was dominated by that futile hope. At that point I knew I could "level up my addictive demand" to a "preference" and still be lovable.

I could prefer a loving relationship with my husband, but it was impossible to demand it—his addiction made it impossible at the time.

But I realized that his love did not determine me. I determined myself. God's love determined me. My spiritual self determined me. Nothing else. I would prefer his human love, but that was no longer most important to me. I was myself—with or without my lover.

This awareness was the breakthrough I needed. First I am united to God, then to my husband. My first love is centered in God. My next is centered in another human.

What a revelation! It had been a long time in coming. What freedom I felt!

The end of the withdrawal period of coaddiction comes when the codependent person finds self and returns to God. It is a place of freedom, a place of joy, a breaking away from the limits of the material world into a more spiritual place. It is a place of release from denial, obsession, and compulsive behavior into a realm of forgiveness, health, and new beginnings.

CHAPTER

THREE

The Shame-Based Family; the Spiritually-Centered Family

Where does sexual addiction and coaddiction begin? Where does it have its roots? It does not suddenly spring up full-grown in adulthood. It is nurtured in the family of origin. The family system produces children like itself.

Addicts and coaddicts share common faulty beliefs which their parents generated. If the tone and temper of the home is shame-based, it will produce a shame-based product. If the tone and temper of the family is spiritually-centered, it will produce children of God. We are all children of God but not all parents project that truth to their children.

In her book, *Back From Betrayal: Recovering From His Affairs* (Center City, Minnesota: Hazelden Publishing Group, 1988), Dr. Jennifer Schneider emphasizes that the codependency in the addict and coaddict precedes the addiction. Both parents start out as codependents in an unhealthy family. It is not unreasonable that if your family does not provide for spiritual growth and self-esteem, you might look outside of yourself to others for your identity. Shame-based families produce codependent children who are looking for love in all the wrong places. Until they reach recovery, they will repeat this search for love, identity, and fulfillment again and again.

In his book, *The Family* (Deerfield Beach, Florida: Health Communications, Inc., 1988), John Bradshaw stresses that families are dynamic social systems with structural laws, components, and rules. What the parents believe about human life will govern the way they raise their children. Parenting forms a child's core beliefs. In our families, we first learn about our selves through our parents' eyes. We learn what feelings are, how to express them, and what feelings are appropriate or inappropriate.

In a shame-based family, we notice a need to idealize and a need to minimize. Children idealize an ineffective parent. Not to do so would give them no parent at all. They minimize behaviors that are unacceptable in order to keep up the pretense of normalcy. Finally, they dissociate from the whole situation and make the determination not to feel anything at all.

Addictions and coaddictions are mood-altering compulsions that sometimes make life bearable. For children in shame-based families, to face the truth of their situation might be more than they can bear. So they learn to escape, to deny, to transfer, to block out, to compensate, to look outside of self—anything but to accept what is right there in front of them.

If there is abuse or any kind of addiction in a family, there is shame. The children learn to defend themselves with ego defense mechanisms. They repress their feelings, deny reality, displace and transfer their rage, and create illusions of love and connectedness.

If it all begins in the family of origin, then we need to look at the family and evaluate what happened there to deal with sexual addiction. For the sake of comparison, let us look at the shame-based family as an unhealthy place and the spiritually-centered family as a healthy place of growth and promise. We do not look back to the family as a way of blaming others or to judge family members but merely to understand what happened in the formation of the addict and the coaddict.

Generally, sex addicts and coaddicts live in shame-based structures as youths. They bring this experience to their adult relationships. Let us look at some general characteristics of both the shame-based family and the spiritually-centered family. In this comparison the origins of sexual addiction and coaddiction will be more evident.

THE ATMOSPHERE IN A SHAME-BASED FAMILY

Where there is a secret in a family, there is a need to deny the truth of it. All kinds of situations may call for keeping a secret. The most basic is *what will the neighbors think?*

Control is primary in a shame-based family. There is a need to control the information that others obtain about the family. There may be rigid rules about keeping all family business within the family. There is a sense of shame about the secret. If the secret is alcoholism, the family denies, rationalizes, and says it really isn't that bad. If the secret is sexual addiction, social taboos compel the family to hide the truth. Society has grown to understand and accept alcoholism to a degree, but sexual addiction is still a secret addiction. Families with this problem guard their secret tenaciously.

Lack of freedom predominates in a family with a secret; they always have to be on guard. They try to look perfect, but inside they know there is something wrong in the family.

Shame-based families get accustomed to the unpredictable. Extremes are the norm. One finds either a crisis ridden environment or an uneasy truce, a confluence. In a confluent atmosphere, everyone pretends that everything is OK. Expectations are unrealistic, with every member of the family trying to keep peace all of the time. No one wants to say what is really wrong. The father's mistress or the mother's companion and the consequent anger and resentment everyone feels are never mentioned. Children perceive the division between parents and feel they are a part of the lie. No matter how many pleasant words are spoken or how many material possessions are accumulated, the problem does not go away until it is addressed. It is like having a pink elephant in the living room. Everyone walks around the huge creature, pretending it is not there, ignoring its bulk and its oppression. Shame-based families are not free; they are controlled by their secrets.

The extent of a family's freedom is directly determined by the number of secrets it keeps.

The atmosphere of the shame-based family is controlling, rigid, inflexible, secretive, and unpredictable.

In *The Family*, John Bradshaw describes it this way: "Shame governs the entire family. The rigid roles are cover-up defenses against the shame core. Each person is hiding and each is afraid to be his true self. All feel abandoned and alone at the deepest level. This shame is inherited generationally and is perpetuated through the rigid roles and ego defenses. Shame begets shame." (p. 72)

In this atmosphere, parents often act in a shameless way even in the face of their own shame. Children growing up in this shame-based environment experience confusion laced with inconsistencies and double messages. They do not develop a strong sense of self because they do not have the proper atmosphere to grow spiritually. In contrast, let us look at the atmosphere of a spiritually-centered family.

THE ATMOSPHERE
IN A SPIRITUALLY-CENTERED FAMILY

The atmosphere in a spiritually-centered family is free. There is no sense of tension and rigid rules, yet there is appropriate discipline.

Family members strive for personal improvement without perfectionism. They understand themselves as children of God using their gifts to do God's will. Letting go of what is beyond their control, they work to improve the things they can control.

It is OK not to be perfect in a spiritually-centered environment; it is understood that God does not judge in the same way the world judges. Different standards govern a spiritual environment. For instance, imperfection is acknowledged as a condition that can produce humility and act as a great motivator.

Imperfection can exist without shame. It is a matter of perspective! In a shame-based family, the chief preoccupation is the addiction while in a spiritually-centered family, the chief motivator is God. The family is God directed.

Each person in the family has great value because each is a precious child of God. Children imbibe a spirit of self-love and self-worth.

Parents who do not focus on living through each other, who do not place ego enhancement and needs gratification before personal spiritual growth, rear children who strive to grow in the same way. In this healthy atmosphere, children learn to be independent individuals and are taught not to waste their gifts, not to waste their time and energy pleasing others and searching for love. There is more quality time for children when codependence is absent.

Spiritually-centered families foster codependency with God, the primary parent.

Openness is the feature of the spiritually-centered family. No secrets! Children are invited to be honest and to speak the truth as they see it. They are made accountable in this environment because there are no loopholes, or mysteries. Rules are clearly set. Personal self-discipline is rewarded.

The spiritually-centered family lives in a *predictable* atmosphere. It has traditions; promises are kept. The family can build together and grow together. They also can grow individually.

Expectations are realistic in this healthy environment. No one is asked to do more than his or her share, and things seem fair most of the time. Children do not assume the role of a parent and parents do not act like children.

Personal boundaries are clear in this atmosphere because personal respect is present. Children can be themselves and still be a part of the family. They are free to concentrate on their own development, and have space and help from the family. Their family nurtures positive values and encourages them to process their own decisions so as to own them personally.

A spiritually-centered family is a fine-tuned workable unit; it is a system that is predictable and propelled by attention to care and love of God, self, and others. Each person is free within the structure but bound in a healthy loyalty to the system. This system nurtures spiritual growth.

The spiritually-centered family is not without boundaries or discipline. In a sense it has more limits because, as a child of God, a person cannot be abused, neglected, or ignored. Child and parent will treat one another with respect and caring attention.

RELATIONSHIPS IN A SHAME-BASED FAMILY

Hypervigilance characterizes relationships in a shame-based family. Members watch other members of the family, of society—everyone. After all, there is a secret to keep.

When others notice this hypervigilance and suspect a problem or respond to it in a negative way, the codependents blame them. The problem, they insist, is not with the family. After all, if they admit to having a problem, they might have to solve it.

Denial is integral to any addiction. Truth may bring social censure. This fear is great in sexual addiction since society has little tolerance or understanding about the disease. Consequently, family control is tight. Relationships are strained and have little flow of energy, little spontaneity.

In their book, *Reclaiming Our Lives, Hope for Adult Survivors of Incest* (Boston, Massachusetts: Little, Brown and Company, 1989, p. 17), Carol Poston and Karen Lison describe shocking cases of incest in which the father violates the daughter and yet presents a perfectly normal picture to the world. The mother simply steps out of the way so that it can all happen. Sometimes parents like these purport radical moral reform in society while in their own homes they keep a terrible secret. A home like this is fodder for intergenerational sexual addiction, so hidden yet so prevalent within our society.

Since incest is a hidden abuse, statistics are hard to verify. According to Poston and Lison, it is suspected that one out of five women is a victim of incest. They cite various authorities who estimate the range from ten to twenty-five million. Most of the cases reported apply to women but in self-help groups across the country many men are speaking out as incest victims.

Relationships in a home suffering from sexual addiction are usually based on conditional love. Everything is a bargain. If you do something for me, I'll do something for you.

The persons involved in the primary relationship in the home—the parents—hold the faulty core belief that sex is the most important sign of love and the most important need.

Children growing up in this environment learn that love has conditions. Later in life they look for partners who believe as they do. The addiction goes on.

In a conditional relationship, needs will not always be met. There is a vacuum of intimacy since intimate needs are not expressed to someone who might be evaluating whether or not they wish to satisfy those needs. The codependent might wait until the proper moment or avoid the risk of being denied by not asking at all.

In a shame-based family, the individual is lost to the family unit. Since there is sacrifice to be made, the family comes first, not the individual.

There is less stability in a shame-based family's relationships. If needs are not being met, the search for another relationship begins. This is the pattern in addiction.

Addiction tears the fabric of a relationship. It causes dysfunctional relationships. A home where there is sexual addiction may experience separation, divorce, and divisiveness between parents. Children who live in these conditions learn to expect instability in their own adult relationships.

No family is perfect, but some function better than others. Any given family is as sick as its weakest member. The level of health is vastly different in every family system.

Unhealthy family systems are like an unbalanced mobile. So much energy goes into making up for the lack of balance in the sick member that all lives become affected. No one is exempt. If both parents are sick, the children will ultimately lose their balance as they make up for the sickness of the parents. In sexual addiction, both parents are preoccupied and consumed with the obsession and compulsion of the disease.

As is so often the case in addiction, the children become the innocent victims of the force that disturbs the family.

RELATIONSHIPS
IN A SPIRITUALLY-CENTERED FAMILY

In a free and open family, a healthy detachment characterizes relationships. Members concentrate on development of self rather than on the family dysfunction. Everyone uses his or her God-given gifts to the fullest. Love is unconditional. There are no demands for love; it simply flows between members. Members affirm one another as they produce and accomplish by using their own special talents. When one falters, another picks up the slack; when that one falters, the favor is returned.

In the spiritually-centered family needs are met. There is no bargaining for love. When the need is there, someone will fill in. It is not planned; it just happens. Family members realize that they can expect steadfast, long-term relationships. Parents or other family members are there for them.

In a spiritually-centered family, the parents are diligent in their roles as mother and father and act appropriately. In a spiritually-centered family, the children, too, are diligent in their roles and act appropriately. The spiritually-centered family fosters relationships that have intrinsic dignity. As children of God, all people deserve respect. In a healthy environment, each person can give love fully and without condition.

RESULTS OF LIVING IN A SHAME-BASED FAMILY

In the shame-based family individual needs are sacrificed to the family dysfunction. It becomes difficult to establish and maintain an individual identity. Children grow up with a distorted sense of self.

The first result of living in a shame-based family is a loss of iden-

41

tity. Rather than hearing positive messages of love, security, acceptance, discipline, guidance, independence, protection, and faith, children hear negative messages. "You are not loved, you are not protected, you are unacceptable, you are not expected to be definitive, you should not rely on direction, you are not separate, you can't have faith in anything." These negative messages cause children to develop a distorted sense of self.

If children are not loved, how are they to feel lovable? Where do they look for that love? To others, outside of self. If children are not safe in their own family, where do they go to find safety? To an outside place.

In a home with sexual addiction, children get negative messages from the negative core beliefs of the addict and the coaddict. Parents communicate the idea that sex is a most important need and that sex can buy love. The emphasis on sex in the home tells children that they must value it too. Later, children take these messages into adult life. Sexual addiction can be intergenerational because the core beliefs that fuel the addiction are passed on. If incest is present in the home, the negative message about the importance of sex is more dramatic.

Children are not able to evaluate these messages as negative or positive. They simply hear them and assimilate them into their being.

The second result of living in a shame-based family is the acquisition of a "disabled will." Contamination of the children's mind with faulty negative messages can seriously disable adult children's decision making ability when it comes to sex and love. Children who grow up in families that overemphasize sex may...

- make faulty decisions regarding trust in relationships
- attempt to control what can't be controlled—staying in a destructive relationship and hoping the mate will change, or leaving it but trying to be friends
- be impulsive, gullible
- see everything in extremes, in black and white—*You love everything about me, you don't love anything about me, I love everything about you, I have no love at all.*
- believe sex must be perfect
- believe romantic, physical contact is the grand experience and life cannot be lived without it.

Children brought up in a shame-based family have trouble aligning their will with the will of God. They have trouble because their identity is distorted and all attempts to correct this distortion come from outside forces—others.

One codependent expressed it this way: "When you know something is wrong inside you and you don't quite know what it is, you try to fix it. You have been taught that sex is a very important sign of love so you want to make that a part of your life. You want someone to desire you so that you know you are lovable. It doesn't occur to you that it might be better if this person emulated you, respecting your wisdom or prudence."

Many adults brought up in shame-based families make poor choices of partners and cause further chaos in their lives. Unhealthy relationships have their own way of producing additional shame. There is conflict, there is loss. More children are born who become victims of shame-based families. The cycle goes on.

Sometimes when the romance dies and spirituality is lacking, divorce occurs. Divorce may occur again when the pattern is repeated. All shame-based losses create more sense of failure, more shame.

The third result of living with so much shame is spiritual bankruptcy. Spirituality is rooted in an established sense of self, a deep love of self as a child of God. People who have heard positive messages of love, security, acceptance, discipline, guidance, independence, protection, and faith will often have a deep spirituality. Spiritual people are alive to life and yet are peaceful. Their will is functional and not disabled. They experience individual growth as well as unity with God.

Spiritually-bankrupt people cannot go inside themselves to find the self love and acceptance they need. Their parents have not helped them to know it is there. It is only through searching that the spiritually-bankrupt people find their way to peace and productivity.

The fourth and final result of living in a shame-based family is the loss of peace and productivity—an absence of joy. In the search for self, an ashamed person will feel disunity. This person cannot live comfortably because he or she feels out of sync with self, others, and God. A certain disquietude, a noticeable unrest might be the legacy of the child of the shame-centered family.

43

When there is unrest, people lose the ability to produce at their very best. But what is more alarming is that their lives seem to be without joy. Never having known real joy, many children of shame-based families live a joyless adulthood also.

RESULTS OF LIVING
IN A SPIRITUALLY-CENTERED FAMILY

The first result of living in a spiritually-centered family is that all members have an established identity. They have been given a wonderful, positive legacy as children of God.

It is easier for children to establish a clear identity when everyone in the home is valued equally as a precious child of God. Children are not merely a material commodity of the marriage; they also have great value and equal worth.

In a spiritually-centered family there is no codependency because each identity is already perfectly formed, needing only to blend with the other members. This does not mean there are no limits or discipline. It may mean more boundaries because when a person sees others as children of God, then he or she cannot abuse, neglect, or ignore them. If others see that person in the same way, then that person will be respected, cared for, and noticed.

All members of spiritually-based families have a divine likeness that is recognized by the parents and established in the children.

The second result of living in a spiritually-centered family is an "able free will." Children brought up in a free-flowing environment where there is respect, equality, openness, and love have a greater chance of developing good decision-making skills. They will not be marred by the negative core beliefs that dysfunctional families carry. They will recognize the positive elements of relationships and respond to what they know. Persons with the same positive qualities will be chosen as partners and associates. Likeness attracts likeness.

Decisions are based on positive values of freedom and responsibility. The ultimate result is spiritual growth.

The third result of living in a spiritually-centered family is peace, productivity, and joy. When spiritual growth is fostered, peace and productivity coexist in the midst of everyday living. Peace does not necessarily mean an absence of conflict or change, but the sense of a higher purpose beyond the activity of living.

To live in the joy of God's will means to have a purposeful life and to be at peace. Children sense this inner peace. It brings them joy, too.

A spiritually-centered home is a joyful place. It may be hectic and full of energy, but it is also full of joy as each member grows in his or her own special way, as God wishes.

A spiritual place is a place of affirmations—parent to parent, parent to child, child to parent. Affirmation brings joy.

Children of God experience a sense of unity with self and offer that spirituality to others. Spirituality comforts and sustains people in the face of hardship. God's children are unmarked by shame—they are functional and free.

Recovery for any person a shame-based family touches comes in the form of a spiritual awareness, a removal of shame. God's grace replaces the shame, making the person functional and free. Then and only then can the person live as a child of God in spiritually-centered family groups.

CHAPTER

FOUR

Denial

One of the key symptoms of any addiction is denial. Denial fuels the sex addict, keeping the addiction active. While denial is alive and well in the addict, it is also alive and well in the coaddict. In fact, the denial of the coaddict enables the addict to continue rationalizations. That is the cruel irony of this love addiction.

How do coaddicts become enablers for the addict? First, they deny behavior, which causes impaired thinking. Secondly, they deny feelings, which causes impaired emoting.

DENIAL OF BEHAVIORS
LEADS TO IMPAIRED THINKING

The first way to deny is by dismissing behaviors that are obviously happening. There is a cycle of behaviors in sexual addiction that clearly marks the disease. You may recall these behaviors noted in chapter one.

• Sexual preoccupation
• Ritualization of action
• Compulsive behaviors
• Despair and hopelessness
• New sexual preoccupation

As this predictable cycle unfolds, the coaddict stands outside the circle and looks the other way. The coaddict simply does not acknowledge what he or she sees. Let us look at each stage.

In the first stage of sexual addiction, the addict becomes pre-occupied with someone else. The addict may need time to think about and fantasize about the new love. A mental distancing or preoccupation is the first sign of a new interest.

An obvious example of this preoccupation might be the addict staying up very late at night or taking long drives alone. An inordinate amount of time alone can signal that the addict is in the initial stages of the cycle of addiction. The coaddict begins to feel general uneasiness about the addict and notices that the addict is present physically but absent mentally. If this situation occurs often, it signals a problem.

The coaddict denies this preoccupation. To acknowledge it would mean there might be another man or woman and, if there is an other man or woman, the relationship might end and the coaddict be alone.

The path of impaired thinking leads the coaddict into a denial of the whole problem. But how can a person live with someone who is preoccupied and not notice it?

Generally, the coaddict suffers from low self-esteem and quickly concludes that the partner's preoccupation shows a lack of interest. Rather than blaming the addict, the coaddict accepts the blame and tries to be a better wife or husband. In essence, the addict gets an immediate payoff for his or her inattention to the partner—a more attentive partner.

The second characteristic of the cycle of addiction is ritualized action. As the addict becomes interested in his or her new love, the partner watches the affair develop. If it has happened before, the coaddict often can predict the person and the pattern of actions.

Watching the inevitable happen is a torturous occupation for the coaddict. It can cause severe discomfort and dysfunction. While the addict is addicted to his or her next love affair, the coaddict is addicted to the partner.

* * *

The church was dimly lit. As Jenny approached the sanctuary she made her usual introductions and spoke in platitudes. As the minister's wife, she had come to understand the words "platitude and amenities" as a natural part of every social event. She smiled automatically.

Polly, the white-haired woman with the lovely smile, was waiting for her at the door.

"I thought you might like someone to sit next to," she said.

"O.K." Jenny said as she touched Polly's arm in a measure of gratitude. These public church services were difficult alone. Bill was to deliver the sermon on this Thanksgiving Day. He was the newest minister in town and that was the custom.

Jenny left him downstairs where he put on his black clerical robes, white collar, and the cross. There was lots of ceremony, lots of tradition in their life. It was good, she thought, yet she was uneasy.

Polly chatted in her usual friendly tone trying to reiterate her feelings for the new minister and his wife.

"You know we are so happy to have Bill with us," she said, adding as an afterthought,"...and you, too." She reached over to touch Jenny's hand.

As they talked in the first pew, the members of the congregation filtered in. Bill made the final adjustments on his robe, gathered up the pages of his sermon, and walked up the worn stairs.

Just as he turned the corner to enter the narthex, he saw Laura. Ever since the special musical the choir had performed, he hadn't been able to put her out of his mind. He had taken her home and made love to her. His heart pounded when he saw her.

At the Women's Fellowship meeting last Monday, she met him by the buffet table. Their arms encircled and he felt her breasts touch his side. Later, she came over to sit next to him. It didn't matter that Jenny was in the room or that the rest of the women were watching.

There was an excitement about her that he couldn't explain. He felt it when she sang a solo or when she took the lead in the church musical. She radiated an electric, dynamic vitality coupled with a subtle, sensual loneliness. Somehow it did not matter that Jenny was at the Fellowship meeting; she would soon leave to go to another meeting. All that mattered was that Laura reached out to touch him.

Bill wondered if Jenny would notice her tonight, but he had to concentrate on the service.

Laura noticed how dimly lit the church was. It fueled her feelings of loneliness. She wished that she had caught a glimpse of Bill. Jenny, she noted, was in the front row with Polly as usual.

I really don't like Jenny, she thought. I really think she is too pos-

sessive and demanding—just too staid. I wish he was free.

"Hello Jim," Bill said in a hoarse whisper as he grasped Reverend Peterson's hand. "It's good to see you."

Nervously, the members of the clergy waited until the sanctuary was filled. Bill looked to see where Laura was sitting. She looked so desolate and alone in her side seat. Her amber hair was curled and loose as usual, and her coat was unbuttoned.

He concentrated on remembering the way she looked the night he undressed her. He wished Jenny would wear silk underwear like Laura did.

When the procession started, Bill watched to see if Laura was looking in his direction. She looked down at the palms of her hands.

Bill's sermon was powerful, well delivered, and poignant—perfect for a Thanksgiving service. Polly clutched at Jenny's hand as Bill made his final remarks. She whispered, "Bill is such a good man, Jenny, such a good man."

For a moment Jenny firmly believed what Polly said. That feeling carried her to the end of the service and down the aisle to the receiving line of clergy at the back of the church.

Halfway down the aisle, Jenny met her close friends, Jack and Mary. They both hugged her. Excitedly, they talked about the next time they would get together. Acting as moderator of the church, Jack was an energetic, thirty-one-year-old man with a wonderful heart. Somehow Jenny sensed that he knew things were not peaceful at the parsonage. Mary was perky and bubbly. Jenny felt supported by these two friends.

The line moved slowly. The conversation began to drag. Suddenly, Jenny caught sight of the amber curls in front of her. It was Laura!

Oh God, she thought, *do I have to go through this again? I just won't look. Yet I really need to know.* Her mind raced. Laura would be reaching Bill soon.

All of the wonderful thoughts his sermons had generated dissipated in that moment. Jenny looked to her side and saw Phil, Bill's best friend. Their eyes met and connected in a look of disbelief as the two of them glanced at Laura and Bill and then back to each other. They both sighed at the same moment. Phil touched Jenny's shoulder in a supportive way.

As Laura had moved up the line, she felt a tenseness in the pit of her stomach. She rehearsed what she would say to Bill. There was so little time. Would she reach out and kiss him as other women were doing? She would try.

Taking Bill's hand and looking directly into his eyes she spoke in a whisper. "I am thankful for your love."

A frightened yet passionate look crossed Bill's face. Jenny saw that look and cringed.

Impulsively, Laura kissed Bill's cheek and felt his heavy robe touch her chest. As she pulled away, he pulled her back and hugged her in a sensual way. She was excited and speechless.

Holding her soft hand, he said, "I missed you the other night. Got caught at a meeting.

"That's OK," she said, even though she hadn't thought so at the time. Once again Bill held her hand in an intimate way and wished her "a wonderful turkey day." Jenny, meanwhile, felt all these gestures in her mind, heart, and the pit of her stomach.

When it came time for Jenny to greet her husband, she was polite but cold. Bill lurched forward, pulling her awkwardly toward him as if she must kiss him in public. Afterward, she fled down the stairs.

It is ironic that, although the ritualized actions of the person addicted to romance cause the coaddict to become preoccupied, the codependent partner still denies the seriousness of the problem. The coaddict thinks that if he or she gets in there and does something about the situation, or does nothing, then the situation will change or go away. But it never does. As long as the addict is active, the addictive cycle will go on.

It is difficult to deny the ritualized actions of the addict; this is because the actions are repeated. But what happens is that the accuser looks foolish in the accusation. For instance, every Tuesday night at 8:30, Joe goes out for ice cream. Going out for ice cream seems fine, but he goes *every* Tuesday night at 8:30 even in the middle of the winter. His wife suspects that someone else also shows up for ice cream.

A husband or wife who accuses a spouse of an affair simply because he or she goes out for ice cream may appear overly possessive. So the coaddict begins to rationalize, convinced that he or she is being oversuspicious. The coaddict has set up a sincere delusion.

The delusion is that the addict is *not* having an affair and that the coaddict is overreacting. Meanwhile, the addict continues to go out

51

every Tuesday night at 8:30 with the hope of meeting the blond from work. This merry-go-round of denial, rationalization, and sincere delusion is the madness of sexual addiction.

The third characteristic of sexual addiction shows up in the exercise of compulsive behaviors. There are times when the addict seems drawn into behaviors that cannot be controlled. It takes time—blocks of time, periods of several hours and days—to act out compulsive sexual behaviors. One of the rights that the addict will fight to preserve is his or her right to those blocks of away time.

We all need space and time but the addict needs it more than most people. The addict needs to be able to disappear for a few hours without any questions asked. In order to arrange and protect these blocks of time, the addict will omit telling all the details of the day.

Compulsive sexual behaviors lead to other behaviors. These include:

- Omissions about certain activities, people, segments of time
- Lying about behavior and whereabouts
- Selectively sharing; lack of spontaneous, honest sharing
- Setting traps such as leaving a trail so spouse's reaction can be controlled

This is the way it might work. Day after day, the addict reports every move. Then suddenly the addict fails to report a whole segment of time. This move throws the coaddict off for awhile. When the coaddict jumps in and questions the addict, he or she has a good excuse.

What the coaddict does not know is that after this question and answer day, there is a free day when the addict can act out his or her compulsive behavior.

Rationalization begins when the coaddict accuses the addict wrongly. The coaddict says, "I was wrong all along. I will never question you again." That may last a day or even a week—just enough time for the addict to act out the compulsive sexual behaviors.

The coaddict's denial is generated by the uncertainty of compulsive behaviors. They are tenuous and predictably uncertain—just the way the addict wants to keep it.

* * *

Jack thought he was going crazy. His wife always collected matchbooks from hotels and restaurants. Her compulsion to collect these matchbooks had reached the stage of a fetish. She was so determined that, on the way out of a restaurant, she would always reach for the matches or even ask the waitress for some. If Katherine were not involved in a pattern of multiple affairs, this behavior would not seem so strange. But why would a woman with a history like this be making a collection of the places she visited?

Jack could tell where Katherine had gone by the matches she carried in her pockets. When he suspected infidelity, he compulsively began to keep track of the matchbooks. Ironically, he had entered into compulsion by living with it. He became obsessed with the matchbooks.

Whenever Katherine left matchbooks on the table, Jack would mentally recall if she had told him about being there recently. Had she been there with him? Was it a hotel? Where was it? Jack was controlled by Katherine's matchbooks and, subconsciously, that was exactly what she intended.

When Katherine wanted an angry response from Jack, she would leave a book from a strange hotel on the table and Jack would respond. His sullenness, anger, or questions would soon force a confrontation and Katherine would respond with a logical explanation.

Once the trap had been set and sprung, Jack was caught. Now he thought it was his fault and for a few days he rationalized his situation and stopped asking questions. On those days Katherine met Henry at the local motel where she did not pick up any matchbooks.

DENIAL OF ABUSIVE SEXUAL ACTIONS

The sad part of sexual addiction is that it can cause severe questions about sexual identity in both participants. Compulsive behavior is not directed by reason and can have little meaning. Yet it may represent within the mind of the partner meaningful sexual interest. To be so deluded is confusing and tragic.

Mary, a coaddict who chose to leave her addictive relationship, recalls the sexual abuse by her husband, Harry. "I always felt I was being compared to someone else. It was as if he was an ancient trader with all his women on different shelves. As he took each one out to

53

use, he would evaluate her particular usefulness that day, that hour. There was never any peace being connected with him because he was the prize and we all paid for his favor.

"Right from the beginning I felt sexually compared. There was something in his manner that said, 'You are being judged and I better like your performance or I'll find someone else.' He evaluated the purchase of a car in the same way, by a very exact process of elimination. One woman could provide prestige, one could make him laugh, one could help financially, and one could be there for emotional support. We were just objects to be used for a certain pleasure. There is a big difference between giving of yourself to please your love, and being compared.

"In order to keep so many partners, there had to be some kind of abusive control going on. Harry was able to be involved with, to use or to be used sexually by five or six women at once. That was not unusual for him. And it involved a pattern of deceit, omissions, and cover-ups.

"No matter how many times he was discovered, even when he lost his job due to promiscuity, he never seemed to recognize the harm he was doing to each individual woman. Why? Well, until I left him, no woman had ever left. How could he know it was unacceptable when all the major players kept playing?

"It became important that I make clear why I left. That was difficult because I was so addicted to him that I drifted back and wavered. The wavering did not leave a clear message and destroyed my credibility."

I recall another story when I read Mary's words. A small child kept a precious, small white stone in a special place for years. One day, in an act of love, the child decided to give it away, presenting it hesitantly to a loved one.

The loved one looked at it and said, "This is a nice stone but it has a black spot in it. Can you get that black spot out?"

The child took it to the sink and brokenheartedly scrubbed and scrubbed the white stone with the black spot, but couldn't get it out. So she covered it up with some white paint and brought it back, transformed, changed from the original.

The painful fact is that the loved one did not like the original white stone and wanted to change it. The little white stone could never be good enough for the loved one.

When a person presents himself or herself sexually to a loved one,

54

it is essential to be a most beautiful white stone. Even if there are hundreds of black specks on the surface, a loved one does not note them. A loved one accepts the expression of love as the greatest gift —a spiritual gift, a gift of self.

Abuse from a sexually addicted partner can be so subtle that it sometimes goes unnoticed. After all, the loving words are there, the actions are there, and all seems so loving. But why doesn't the co-addict feel good enough? When you feel you are being constantly compared to others, it is difficult to be good enough.

The final symptom of the sex addict is evidenced in bouts of despair and a sense of hopelessness. A sex addict seeks that perfect union, the connection that will make him or her complete. Since it is impossible to ever find that connection, a sense of ultimate defeat is faced.

In *Looking for Love in All the Wrong Places* (New York: Avon Books, 1988), Jed Diamond observes that the addict learns to hate the lover who can never give enough and learns to hate self for being so dependent. The rage turned inward can cause the addict to become depressed or even suicidal.

Usually, both addict and coaddict are broken people who feel they are out of union with themselves, others, and God. That feeling, momentarily stilled by romance, can cause great despair. This is true even though the addict and coaddict appear charming, lovable, and even charismatic. The examples of many public figures come to mind.

Addicts must always come back to periods of despair and hopelessness. This despair creates the hangover for the addict and drives the addict on to a new sexual conquest.

Generally, sex addicts are not satisfied with themselves, their sexual partners, or their marriages. They are restless. Everyone tries to help them find ultimate happiness. Others "do" for them, love them, stand beside them in their despair.

When the coaddicts are in the helping professions, the needs of the coaddicts may not be so obvious. In a helping environment, coaddicts are allowed to act out their own hopelessness and their situation seems less oppressive. But helping others can be a smokescreen for a very despondent soul.

A teacher friend once recalled a time when she was at the bottom of a pit of despair. Her marriage was hopelessly alcoholic and violent. She was overburdened with three children and the threat of bankruptcy. What did she do? She went back to teaching and became the advocate for every troubled child in her class. In essence, her emotional instability found its own level. Those troubled children of the sixties found their match in her, a very troubled, emotionally disturbed adult.

The denial of the coaddict comes in the delusion that the partner is a good person, not a desperate, despairing person. Denying the addict's despair or taking on the despair perpetuates the life of addiction. Refusing to see the preoccupation, ritualized behavior, compulsive actions, and bouts of despair enable the addict to go on with his or her addiction.

The damage such continuous impaired thinking does to the mind is alarming. The coaddict's sanity cannot be restored until something is done about the addiction. However, doing something requires confrontation, and that takes great courage and insight.

Impaired thinking leads to impaired emoting and a general lack of emotional balance. Once again, the coaddict shows the addict's symptoms along with a sense of despair and hopelessness.

DENIAL OF FEELINGS
LEADS TO IMPAIRED EMOTING

The coaddict caught in a family where sexual addiction is rampant not only dismisses the obvious actions of the addict but also dismisses his or her own intuitive feelings. Reality is distorted.

For example, on the social level the addict may be charming and flattering. He or she appears to be extremely attentive to the partner. Why not? What the world sees is a man or a woman who is "the perfect partner." Everyone finds the addict desirable. But at the personal level there is little or no commitment.

Because of this lack of commitment, the partner feels apprehensive or unusually anxious. Anxiety shows in his or her manner, perhaps in the face or eyes. The coaddict never seems self-assured in social situations because the addict may be making a connection with a new lover.

That realization causes anxiety, frustration, and anger. The coaddict is forced to hide feelings because the world may not understand the problem. It would be difficult for a coaddict to interrupt a party conversation and ask to be excused because he or she thinks the addict is lining up a date. If this is the case, the coaddict gets anxious.

Coaddicts live in a box, an isolated state. Their feelings are not validated and they become the problem when in essence they are involved with someone else's sexual addiction. This is not an easy place for anyone to be. This is not an easy place to be honest about feelings.

Consider anger. When the addict seems purposely late or lies about where he or she has spent the day, what does the coaddict do with anger?

Different situations need different solutions. There is confusion about what feelings are attached to what. Feelings of anger come and go. They are jagged, erratic. The coaddict appears off balance or angry all of the time.

People can't understand how such a charming person (the addict) goes on with such an angry person (the coaddict). The cycle of addiction and coaddiction goes on.

*   *   *

Once again, let's look at Jenny and Bill.

They had hurried to get dressed for the ten o'clock service at church. As usual, she made the coffee and had it ready when he came to the kitchen.

Before he sat down he hugged her. It was an encircling, warm hug that lingered. Then she remembered that her dress needed to be pressed.

"The coffee is right there," she said, pulling a little to the left.

"Where?" he said as he held her firmly in place, touching the small of her back with his hand.

"There," she said, laughing and moving to the right.

"Where?" he said, holding her even tighter in his grip. Again she laughed and pulled away saying, "Oh, Bill."

Bill went to the coffeepot and poured a cup of coffee. Jenny ran upstairs. She pulled her grey and white dress from the closet, then ran downstairs and began ironing it. When Bill saw her coming up the stairs with her slip flying behind her, he whistled.

That scene flashed in her mind later as the congregation sang the processional hymn. Jenny loved the special way Bill touched her. As the order of worship progressed, Jenny noticed Laura slipping into the end seat of the choir section. As usual, her amber hair was loose and unkempt. She looked breathless and excited. After she sat down, she peeked a look at the minister and smiled. He smiled back and her head went down again.

Suddenly a surge of anger overwhelmed Jenny. She became restless. Her friend Mary touched her hand as if sensing her anxiety.

The scripture reading was from the Song of Solomon and the sermon was based on love. Jenny noted that it was direct, almost sensual, and her husband delivered it beautifully, powerfully.

After the benediction, Jenny moved down the aisle and was painfully aware of Laura's presence. Since she was the last member of the choir to process, she was the first to greet Bill. He gave her a long, tender hug and whispered some words to her.

When Jenny got to Bill, she dutifully kissed her husband while the rest of the congregation watched. He hugged her warmly as she complimented him on the sermon. He said, "I love you," and she responded with "I love you, too." For that moment everything seemed fine again. Somehow for Jenny the words "I love you" seemed to cancel out the anger she felt in Laura's presence.

Moving away from the line, Jenny greeted the older members of the parish. She became caught up in conversation as she moved into Fellowship Hall.

But Jenny was still distracted by the intimacy she had witnessed between her husband and Laura. It kept coming back to her. She remembered last Thanksgiving and the Women's Fellowship meeting, and the time she had dropped by the office and found Laura there. She tried to remember what time of day that was. She lost her train of thought and was hardly able to follow the conversation with Mrs. Smallgrove.

Bill, seeing that Jenny was engrossed in conversation with Mrs. Smallgrove, moved over to where several choir members were talking with the director.

Shaking the hand of the choir director, Bill complimented him on the music the choir had sung in the worship. Then he moved over to Laura and put his hand on the small of her back, saying "And your solo was magnificent, dear. It was a magnificent and meaningful experience for me." Blushing, Laura looked at Bill and whispered, "Thank you; your sermon had special meaning for me."

At that moment, Jenny looked around for Bill. She saw him touch Laura in the same place he had touched her that morning. A surge of rage and jealousy went through her. Quickly, Bill turned to the rest of the choir members and paid them a general compliment. Then he moved on to where Jenny was talking with Mrs. Smallgrove. As Bill and Jenny talked to the woman, Bill put his arm around Jenny and touched her back. She pulled away—irritated. Several people nearby, including members of the choir, noted it.

The coaddict caught up in sexual addiction is prey to everyone else's emotions and yet never emotes honestly. If someone tries to steal a person's silverware or TV, that person has a right to get angry. If someone tries to steal another person's husband or wife, that person has a right to get angry. Yet a coaddict is often denied those feelings. The coaddict's situation can't be revealed because of social censure. The coaddict's anger makes him or her appear overly sensitive or jealously petty.

So what happens to this anger? Where does it go? Often, the coaddict swallows the anger and it grows into a deep depression. Once again the coaddict becomes the problem. He or she is the sad one. How can such a happy-faced lover stand being married to such a sad face?

Attached to all loss is a certain amount of sadness. Any grieving process includes sadness. Yet in a dysfunctional relationship the partner is lost even though the partner is still present. The addict appears to be a perfect, attentive lover. The addict seems to do all the right things. Yet the coaddict knows that the addict is preoccupied with someone else. The addict is lost to the primary relationship.

Suffering the grief of a constant, sustained loss over a period of years can do untold damage to coaddicts. After awhile, they are hard-pressed to identify their feelings. Anger and sadness are so interwoven that it may take a good psychologist to help unravel the pieces of the emotional puzzle.

Impaired emoting can become a way of life as the coaddict loses touch with intuitive feelings or simply denies feelings. Impaired emoting eventually causes severe emotional disorder. The confusion of it all causes dissociation from self; the simplest feeling becomes catastrophic. One of the major travesties of sexual addiction is the destruction of healthy emotional responses.

In this state of impaired emoting, the only apparent happiness is sexual. There is a certain joy as the partner reaffirms union with the coaddict. The addict is intent on assuring the coaddict's desirability.

This is what the addict does best—assures a partner of his or her sexuality. However, the cruel irony of the disease is that the coaddict may be one among many sexual partners—each believing he or she is the most desired. It is no wonder the coaddict feels so bad so much of the time. Being denied feelings for a long period causes emotional numbness.

So often the coaddict simply says, "I can't believe this is happening to me." He or she denies what is seen and felt. Eventually, all reality gets distorted. This is where a kind of insanity sets in.

Living with distorted reality can cause a temporary insanity which can lead to sincere delusion. To protect sanity, the coaddict pretends everything is OK. He or she rationalizes impaired emoting and denies sadness, anger, and frustration. He or she begins to say and believe this is not happening to him or her.

Other thoughts are excluded. If any other thoughts were to enter the mind, the coaddict might have to ask why he or she agrees to go on in this unhealthy negative state. He or she may have to ask why it is so abhorrent to admit that a lover is loving others. The feared answer is that the coaddict is not lovable.

The coaddict may have to break the relationship and recognize his or her own sexual dependency upon the addict. That realization may seem more unbearable than the day-to-day mental confusion.

Why does the coaddict deny intuition, feelings, and spiritual being? Why is the coaddict's identity given to another person? Perhaps the sense of self is not as defined as it could be. Perhaps the coaddict questions his or her own sexuality. Whatever the reasons for this denial, if the coaddict is to get well, he or she must break through the denial to the reality of the moment, to the truth of the addiction.

FIVE

Signs of Obsession

Recently I had occasion to observe several couples as they functioned in a group. One couple stood out. They were inseparable; they mirrored each other's actions and attitudes. It was like seeing one person, not two.

Everyone has seen couples like that or perhaps functioned like that in a relationship. On the surface they seem so romantic, but one perceives an unhealthy dependency underneath all the togetherness.

Some questions might be asked about such relationships:

Who gives in?

How often?

On what issues?

Is there an imbalance of power in the relationship?

A partner inordinately obsessed with the other partner thinks about that person most of the time. There is a need to please the partner. It is as if one partner invites that kind of attention while the other responds. Friends, counselors, and clergy who know the couple might be privately concerned, but since the dependency doesn't cause any serious, overt problems, they don't interfere. Codependency is a quiet desperation, a quiet, parasitic sickness.

Once in awhile friends and relatives will try to encourage the addicted partner "to be their own person." They may even invite this partner to do things separately in order to break the pattern of addiction. However, it is not so easily broken.

Several clear-cut signs of obsession accompany sexual co-addiction.

The first sign of obsession is repeated, incessant, conversational references to the loved one. Whatever preoccupies the mind usually preoccupies speech. Therefore, addicts make constant verbal references to their mate.

A well-meaning friend may try to distract an addicted partner only to find the whole conversation returning to the lover. That can be disconcerting for a good friend, especially if the friend is interested in the coaddict and not necessarily the partner. Attempts to change the conversation can be thwarted continuously to the point of frustration. Even mentioning the obsession won't work and may destroy the initial friendship. After all, the addicted person would probably prefer to be with the loved one anyway. It seems a no-win situation; an addictive relationship may interrupt many good friendships.

Mental obsession can be detected by charting the number of references made to the significant other. Therapists and psychologists usually listen carefully to their patients' conversations. Mentioning a husband dozens of times in an hour without mentioning self—except in relationship to the husband—signals mental obsession with another. Obviously that imbalance needs therapeutic attention.

Society gives us permission to get "hooked" on a lover. This intense meshing is seen as a sign of love. Actually, it is a sign of less love or no love at all. Just listen to the words of popular songs: "I don't want to live without you," "I can't live without you, baby," "You're nobody 'til somebody loves you," and "You are my everything." It is big business to propagate romantic love; it has been for years.

Does that mean that addicted lovers are not sincere? Absolutely not. We get caught in the sincere delusion that what we are doing is not only healthy, but the sign of true love.

The more the addict gets involved in the life of the loved one, the more the coaddict spends time and energy on the addict's interests and pursuits. It is hard to think in terms of self when all energy is directed to the other.

Yet, ironically, it is the self that makes a person lovable; it is a person's individuality that creates a love object. Therefore, changing a partner, directing all of the self to that person's interests, makes a person less desirable or, at best, less interesting. A mature love relationship revels in the separateness of the partners. The spice of individuality seasons the relationship.

The second sign of obsession is an overemphasis on sexuality. The myth of sexual addiction is that sex determines love. Consequently, there is an overemphasis on sexual activity within the relationship. One partner is compulsively addicted to sexual situations and the other is struggling to secure a sexual loyalty from their partner. Neither one can win in this addiction. As the addict acts out his or her addiction, the coaddict becomes more preoccupied and more controlling with the addict in an attempt to obtain that sexual fidelity. Thus, there is an exaggerated emphasis on the sexual component of their relationship.

The third sign of obsession is a need to track the conversation of the addict in order to detect untruth. It takes a great deal of time and mental energy to keep track of the lies the addict tells. Inevitably, the lies appear. Since it is impossible for anyone who leads a double life to keep accurate track of it all, that person will eventually be caught in a lie. The first time this happens, the coaddict rationalizes the whole thing, thinking the incident was imagined or the result of an overly suspicious mind.

The addict will do anything to support the thought that the coaddict is inordinately jealous. As long as coaddicts go along with this theory, they will doubt their own reasoning and second guess themselves.

In any addiction, this defensive strategy is the name of the game. Shift the blame! Make the coaddict doubt his or her own observations! Implant self-doubt in the coaddict and no action will be taken.

Much of the time, the coaddict will feel jealous and controlling due to repeated infidelities. When the coaddict is accused of this behavior, defense is difficult because it is true. Yet the coaddict feels great anger because the blame has delicately been shifted.

With the addict, discrepancies always show up in the details of stories. The coaddict learns to keep track of all the details. Keeping track of the details of someone else's life is a time-consuming obsession. However, to the coaddict active in his or her addiction, it seems like a necessary tool for maintaining sanity.

* * *

The Farmington River was high and mighty that day. It was exactly noon when they pulled into the parking lot of the restaurant. She

63

was a little apprehensive about her choice of restaurants. The paint on the old Victorian building was discolored from the sun.

He reassured her. "It is a lovely place, a quality restaurant," he said. She was happy he was pleased with her choice.

"Would you like to sit by the river or go into the dining room?" she asked. He put his hand on her waist and directed her toward the stairs. She complied.

"A lovely room," she said to the waitress as they were seated. And it was a lovely place, a lovely day. The early summer sun shimmered on the river. Wrought iron chairs were in a delightful array beside the water, and lovers strolled here and there. They watched them from the window as they inspected the menu.

Even the name of the restaurant was delightful—Apricots. Fine antiques were in the room which was filled with fresh flowers.

"Look at that vase," she said, motioning to the sideboard.

"That would be beautiful in the bay window at home," he answered. She agreed.

They mused over whether to order eggs Benedict. At the last minute she changed her order to match his. "Why do I do that?" she thought. "Oh well."

The fresh bread was warm and the waitress was attentive to their needs. It was a delightful day and a delightful way to spend a holiday afternoon.

They talked about work and the kids and all the ordinary things. Ordinary things seemed to take on extraordinary meaning in an extraordinary place.

"I saw Walt this week," he said. "I was so impressed. He made an effort to call and tell me that he has turned his life around and things are going great for him."

"Oh," she said.

"Yes. Last October he met someone new and he is very happy. This is the first time I've seen him in over a year and he was so anxious to tell me all the news."

"Oh," she said.

Suddenly the Victorian dining room lost its charm. The apricots stenciled on the post by the door, the vases of blossoms on the sideboard lost their beauty. Nancy knew that she had discovered another discrepancy in Frank's repertoire of stories.

She distinctly remembered that in January, after a particularly long day, Frank burst into the house saying he had just spent the day with Walt, who happened to stop by the office. That was January. Frank had just said that when he saw Walt this week it was the first time he had seen him in a year. Frank lied. This August day didn't seem so delightful.

The coaddict is faced with a dilemma when the addict is actually caught in a lie. The problem is whether or not to confront. Confronting a sex addict can be a formidable task.

Surely the lovely day in the story was ruined and Apricots will never be a pleasant place to return. Ironically, the coaddict may be blamed again for being suspicious, controlling, and for ruining the afternoon.

But the reality is that a sex addict cannot cover up the secrets forever without forgetting some of the details. Eventually, the lies erode the relationship and cause a breach of trust.

When the addict is confronted with a lie, he or she usually denies it. Telling the truth would mean having to explain the reason for the lie and, in turn, having to explain where that time really was spent. To avoid this, the addict will inevitably claim he or she never told the coaddict about this, that the coaddict must have imagined the entire thing. The coaddict who is adept at keeping track of details knows there is no chance of being wrong. The coaddict knows the addict lied and knows why. It is a painful experience.

Usually, a situation like this ends in an uncomfortable silence with angry recriminations from the coaddict or self-righteous indignation from the addict. The coaddict feels terrible for not having controlled his or her suspicions. But the bare truth is that the addict lies compulsively to cover the addiction and the coaddict spends time keeping track of the lies.

Sooner or later all trust and spontaneity is lost in the relationship. Many lovely times are lost when the addict lets down, forgets the addiction, gets lost in the moment, and slips into a lie. The coaddict loses many days keeping track of the lies.

A fourth sign of obsession is inordinate sacrifices made in people pleasing. People pleasing leads to an inordinate and unbalanced level of power. The more the coaddict sacrifices, the more power the addict gets.

The sexually addicted person cheats on the relationship, yet the codependent person tries to win the favor of the addict. This doesn't

65

make much sense. Nevertheless, in most cases of sexual addiction, the addict seems to have the upper hand. In reality, he or she is like a frightened child running from place to place to be affirmed with love and affection or with sex, which represents love and affection.

The coaddict chases the little child trying to provide more love and attention so the child will not feel the pain. It is a never-ending cycle of nonfulfillment.

What an extraordinary situation! The addict betrays the coaddict again and again, yet the coaddict's response to that betrayal is to try even harder to please the addict. The coaddict will do anything, give up anything, suffer anything for the love of the addict. The coaddict holds the same core belief as the addict: Sex is the most important sign of love.

Addiction involves a lack of compromise and fairness that exists due to the imbalance of power within the relationship. Anyone outside the relationship can see the situation. The coaddict gives in an effort to control the addict; the addict takes while denouncing the actions of the coaddict.

In any addiction, the wronged partner has a justifiable reason for anger. After all, he or she gave so much and was betrayed. What a reward for noble behavior.

However, recovery shows us that "giving to get" is no more noble than receiving without giving. Love addicts don't have much time or energy to invest in one partner. They are not trying to please anyone, but to survive themselves. Most of the time they end up trying to appease someone. Keeping track of multiple partners is hard work. Most addicts who maintain multiple partners become very adept at juggling their time, energy, and sexual attentions.

Coaddiction resembles a state of deep grief. The addict is lost to the spouse but available to all others. There is no relationship, no marriage. Yet the coaddict cannot affirm that loss. The death exists right there in the house, in the living room and sometimes in the bedroom. The coaddict is not allowed to recognize that loss and go on with the grief.

Coaddicts can become stuck in the early stages of grief, going around in a state of shock, immobilized by emotions. They don't believe what is really happening. To outsiders, coaddicts seem to have the most attentive partner in the world. In reality, they are married to someone who is not emotionally available. They experience grief but can't process it. They feel stagnated and frustrated.

A grieving person resolves pain by acknowledging the loss and reconnecting with others. Coaddicts who acknowledge the loss of a partner seem like complaining, unreasonable people. They become stuck because they are unable to "go public" with their concerns. Sometimes their only escape is within themselves or to another person or addiction. Sometimes they resort to their own self-destructive behaviors as they try to wrest themselves from a constant grieving process. They can try to relieve the pain through alcohol, drugs, or adultery. More often, however, they simply obsess over the addict. They engage in people pleasing in order to establish a better relationship. Since there can be no viable relationship with an addicted person, however, all attempts to establish one are futile. Thus, more and more frustration accompanies the coaddict. Here are some of the things coaddicts do to fix the relationship they think is there but is not.

• Disregarding own needs.
• Overlooking hurtful behavior.
• Covering up behavior which is against values.
• Appearing cheerful when hurting.
• Avoiding conflict to keep up appearances.
• Allowing oneself to be disrespected repeatedly.
• Allowing values to be compromised.
• Faulting self.
• Believing there are no options.
• Living with unacceptable behavior.

The fifth sign of obsession is one-sided bargaining by the coaddict rather than healthy negotiation and compromise. The coaddict can't believe the addict is really lost to him or her. The coaddict fears abandonment and bargains so that the reality of it will not come crashing down.

By disregarding his or her own needs, the coaddict hopes to keep the beloved happy and faithful. The coaddict bargains for the love of the addict. By overlooking the hurtful behavior and even covering it up, the coaddict hopes to keep the beloved from getting angry and repeating the behavior. The coaddict thinks that disregarding or covering up the behavior will stop it. But the behavior only gets worse because it is already out of control. It is compulsive.

The coaddict appears cheerful when hurt and avoids conflict to keep up appearances. If the spouse is in a public position of power, life becomes even more complicated because the coaddict is bargaining a livelihood, social status, and career. The general public does not often accept sexual addiction as a disease even though there are hospitals that treat it.

When the coaddict threatens to expose the sickness, this is a real threat to the financial and social security of the addict. Such leverage and power can make the coaddict a formidable enemy for the addict.

The addict creates enemies in betrayed lovers. Ironically, if a betrayed lover does have the courage to confront the addict, the lover will lose everything he or she is trying to protect.

The coaddict allows standards to be compromised in an effort to bargain, but in doing so loses anyway. The threat to the coaddict is repeated infidelities; the threat to the addict is exposure.

As long as the addiction remains active, bargaining will go on. The coaddict may use a futile but elaborate system of rewards and punishments, financial or sexual. No honest compromise, no real negotiating occurs in such a threatening battle.

* * *

What a long way, she thought. Route 3 on the way to New Hampshire seemed to go on forever. Clare noted it was a five-hour ride. Her mind drifted back to last spring and the financial details of the "almost" sale.

"We could have done it," she said aloud. "The builder would have financed the last $15,000."

As she drove through the beautiful mountains, she realized there wouldn't be another chance like that. Property values had increased since last spring. Clare remembered the way the condo was situated on Echo Lake. She remembered one particular sunset. It was with a touch of sadness that she passed the little shops and the country store. It was with a touch of remorse that she relived the days of indecision while they waited for the bank's decision.

That was the turning point, she thought. Peter might not have turned against her, they might not now be separated if she had said yes to the deal. They might be coming here for a weekend now. She might not be alone if she had been able to make that deal.

Then reason and clarity began to filter into her reminiscing. The clarity was the result of removing herself for four months from the addictive relationship.

The deal would have tied up her retirement fund. She would have been so tied down that she could never have been able to move out. What would have happened if he cheated on her again? She would have had no options if she owned a second home.

As the cars rushed by, she felt a sense of relief. She noted the Beasley Realty sign along the road. *Life is as it should be,* she thought.

Clare, only a few months out of an addictive relationship, had a tendency to second-guess herself. She was going through "what ifs." What if she had done this or that? At a later time she would look back on this scene with incredulity. How could anyone believe that buying a summer house would save a marriage that was already dysfunctional? But even more important, how could Clare think it was her role to jeopardize her future to provide this second home? Conversely, how could her husband allow her to do such a thing, knowing the relationship was marked by repeated infidelities?

The grandest summer house in the world would not fix their problems. It would, no doubt, confuse the situation even more. Clare would have to wonder who he might be taking there.

Coaddicts have a tendency to believe they can buy the loyalty of a lover. Fortunately, loyalty is a gift—given freely. If a person bargains for love, there is no love present.

The final sign of obsession is low self-esteem. When coaddicts bargain for the loyalty of their lover, self-esteem is lost. A person cannot think well of self when he or she believes that self is less important than the most significant person in one's life.

For children brought up in a dysfunctional home, the message of unlovableness is not new. This may have been the primary message received from parents dealing with addictions. But no matter who gives the message or reinforces it, the result is the same. Anyone who hears that they are not worthwhile and believes it does not have self-esteem.

In her book, *Women Who Love Too Much,* Robin Norwood describes in great detail the classic problems of women in a state of obsession where they give too much of themselves. She claims women who love too much have had little nurturing in childhood and try to fill that unmet need by becoming caregivers, especially to men who appear to be needy. These women respond to emotionally unavailable men whom they try to change with love. They are terrified

69

of abandonment and will do anything to keep a relationship from ending. There is no limit to their willingness to help, to wait, or to please. They take more than fifty percent of the responsibility, guilt, and blame in any relationship.

ically low self-esteem and do not believe they deserve to be happy. Rather, they believe they must earn the right to enjoy life. Since they experienced little security in childhood, they control their men. Essentially, they are addicted to men and emotional pain and may be predisposed to other addictions. Generally, they are not attracted to men who are kind, stable, and reliable because nice men seem boring.

So it is with those who love too much, with those who are obsessed with someone else other than themselves and God. So it is with those who become coaddicts.

CHAPTER

SIX

Compulsive Behavior

Anyone caught in a cycle of compulsive behavior feels like he or she is on a merry-go-round. The sex addict obsessed with the good feeling of sexual conquest will have a series of affairs. After awhile, names and faces will change but all will seem the same, like the ride on the merry-go-round.

One member of a twelve-step group for sex addicts spoke about having several women on the same day, even on the same afternoon. It was as if the women had lost any personal identity and he was maintaining a sexual supply to keep things from getting out of control. Sex had become a merely physical act. It had turned on him and really had no meaning. It is analogous to the drunk who gets up in the morning and has a drink because he needs the alcohol to calm his nerves. Even though he does not wish to drink, he does because he has to. That is compulsive behavior.

What about the behavior of the coaddict? Ironically, the partner who observes the addict gets into the same kind of ritualized behavior as the addict. The coaddict becomes as compulsive in attempting to control the addict's new lovers as the addict is in pursuing them. After awhile the behavior is recognizable and the addict is in a cycle, doing the same things with a new lover as with existing ones. That is compulsive behavior.

The coaddict experiences the feeling of being caught in a cycle because the circumstances in which the addict meets the lover are always the same. The lover is always a young woman who looks to her minister for counseling, a coed who looks to a professor for help, or

71

a lonely housewife who looks to the gardener for sexual fulfillment. The lovers are repeats of prototypes that are recognizable to the co-addict.

One member of SAnon told the group that she began to look at her behavior when it seemed all women were a threat to her marriage. In time, she could not distinguish between the women that her husband was likely to be sexually involved with and the women who were just friends or business acquaintances. All women looked like potential affairs—even older, attractive women in their seventies who might provide a grandmotherly image. When it all ran together, she became frightened about her own hypervigilance or her compulsive attention to her husband's activities with females.

In a similar way, an addict might seek help when he or she realizes that the love partners have lost any personal identity.

For the coaddict obsessed with the cycle of the addict, it becomes a pattern of negative, controlling behaviors that have no positive results. Names and faces change but the behaviors stay the same.

When the cyclic motion that compulsive behavior seems to generate is slowed, a discernible pattern evolves. This is the pattern that needs to be examined. Let us look first at the source of the compulsive behavior and secondly, at the results of that behavior.

NEGATIVE SOURCES
OF COADDICT COMPULSIVE BEHAVIOR:
FEARS AND FAULTY BELIEFS

The first source of compulsive behavior for the coaddict may be fear. Fear is very familiar to the codependent. A primary fear is one of abandonment.

The coaddict hangs on tight to the addict precisely because he or she fears the loss of the loved one. The coaddict expects to be abandoned. Ultimately, this is what happens.

This powerful fear appears to be an exaggerated feeling operating out of the faulty belief that the coaddict is not a worthwhile person. If the coaddict were a treasure, a valued child of God, no one would want to abandon him or her. But a worthless person can expect to be abandoned.

What makes sexual addiction so complicated is the coupling of an unnatural yet powerful fear with a faulty belief. Most coaddicts are not unworthy persons who could not attract desirable partners. On the contrary, coaddicts many times are most desirable and are particularly attentive to remaining attractive at any age. So what is it that prompts them to be so afraid of losing a lover? It is the underlying faulty belief, the conviction that they are not worthwhile persons or, perhaps, not worthwhile sexual partners.

Whatever that belief, it is one that invites the sex addicts to act out their addictive behavior.

A person who believes he or she is not a worthwhile individual can easily be convinced to put up with unacceptable behavior because of the fear of abandonment. Sex addicts activate the coaddicts' fear of abandonment and validate their sense of unworthiness.

In the case of separation, it is the coaddict who many times seems to fare the best and effectively reestablishes a life while the addict flounders, roaming from one partner to another. When the cycle gets interrupted, the addict loses control over the coaddict and panic sets in.

Signals and signposts along the way indicate that things are out of control. At times these signs are significant enough to break into the cycle of addiction and provide awareness to the coaddict. Sometimes the coaddict can stop personal addiction by recognizing his or her own insanity.

* * *

Charlene, a forty-five-year-old business woman, was a coaddict. She would sacrifice anything to be loved by James, a handsome, charming professor at the local college. Although actively involved with several women, he still made plans to marry Charlene. Although she suspected his affairs, she accepted his proposal of marriage. Not until she realized where her addiction had taken her did she break her engagement.

As she sped along Route 109, Charlene anticipated the turn onto Route 52 to Dexter, Plymouth, and Scarsdale. She refigured her profit from the last sale yesterday and silently thanked her father for his shrewd business skill.

It had been a week since she'd been home and she thought about James and how special it would be to see him. In just seven months they would be married. Was it really seven months? What about inviting the other professors at Trinity? How should the invitations be handled? Perhaps it should be a general invitation. Maybe they should have a reception in the Main Hall and no one would be left out. She would talk this over with James.

It was a comfortable feeling knowing they would be married during the next calendar year.

"I'll have a dress made," she said aloud.

"—and the rings. I will contact that man who works with gold," she told herself as she drove up to the toll booth. The woman at the toll booth gave her an unfriendly look, but she didn't care. She was happy thinking about how happy she was.

The radio blared as she stepped up the speed. She hardly noticed the bridge crossing over the Agawam River. It was 2:30; she was an hour early.

"I'll go over to James's apartment and surprise him," she continued. "We can be alone for awhile before I go home."

In his office at Trinity University, James was aimlessly shuffling papers from one corner of his desk to the other. The telephone rang. It startled him, but he gained his composure when he heard Ann's voice.

"Sleeping at your desk?" she asked in a suggestive voice.

"Oh, yeah," he said, recognizing her voice and her inference. "Just sleeping, Sweetie."

"That's too bad," she continued with further inference.

Then she shifted to a different, more conversational tone, asking about his day and his new classes. He filled her in with the latest details of his work just as if she were an ordinary colleague.

"What are you doing later today?" she asked with a return to that sensual tone he loved. For a moment he visualized being with her at her apartment. Then he thought of Charlene. She would be home for the weekend.

"Charlene is coming in," he said with a heavy voice.

"Then, I will have to behave with your fianceé around."

"Yes," he said, stabbing at the ashtray with the butt of the cigarette he had just put out. He recognized a slight feminine tapping at the door.

"Excuse me, someone is here," he whispered into the phone. Getting up from his desk, he quietly opened the door for his student Katie. She was the delicate one, the one having so much trouble in his class, the one who needed special tutoring.

"Come in, dear," he said. Timidly, she smiled at him and sat down on the sofa.

74

"Yes, I have to go," he said into the phone.

"Reluctantly, I hope," Ann retorted at the other end of the line.

"Of course, of course," he answered in mock agitation.

"Good-bye, dear. I will call you." Katie smiled up at him from place across the room.

Silently, James took his place on the sofa beside his student. He reached out to touch her shoulder. She resisted and immediately opened her book.

"What is wrong?" he asked—irritated.

"Nothing!"

"What is wrong?" he persisted.

After a long pause Katie said, "You're getting married. I told you about that in my letter. Did you get my letter? I just can't go on, James. That's why I wrote you that letter."

"Yes, I got it and it was beautiful—like you," he said touching her face.

With a note of resignation in his voice and a look of understanding in his eyes, he moved away from her and began the lesson.

At the end of the lesson she lingered, telling herself that it was alright to kiss him good-bye. Then she left almost as quietly and gently as she had come in.

James looked at the disheveled desk and sighed. He lit a cigarette and gathered up his notes and papers, stuffing them into his briefcase. Charlene would be there in an hour and he must go home.

The phone rang but he didn't answer it. *I can't be bothered with Ann,* he thought.

As Charlene unlocked the front door of James's apartment, she almost dropped the flowers in her arms. Some brown-eyed Susans fell from the bunch and landed on the porch. She struggled to get them and dropped some more.

Across the street, Mrs. Warren watched with interest. She always watched. She knew that Charlene was a "new" girlfriend and she wondered if she knew about the others that came from time to time. Probably not, the woman thought. He's going to get into trouble someday. She was sure of that.

Once inside the apartment, Charlene dropped the flowers into the open sink. They fell in a disarray of color and loose stalks. Some fell on the floor.

"I guess I'd better put these in a vase."

She was unable to locate one in the cupboard. Then she noticed a bunch of dried-up flowers on the kitchen table.

"Great, I'll use this," she said as she anticipated James's delight at the fresh flowers on the table. Quickly she pulled the dead flowers from the white vase. When she tried to put them into the garbage pail, they wouldn't fit. She took the lid off and pressed them into the bucket. Just as she did, she noticed a greeting card and a torn up letter.

Compulsively, she took it from the trash and scrutinized the handwriting. Almost immediately she felt a sharp pain in the pit of her stomach. It was as if someone had kicked her. She didn't want to see this letter but she knew she must.

Piecing it together, she read the words "...love in my heart" and then, "for you." It was clearly a love letter and she had to know who sent it. More pieces "...when we make love" and "...when you look into my eyes." My God! She was stunned and shaken. The postscript was dated the day before.

"How could he do this?" she screamed as she paced the room. Feverishly she continued to piece the final parts of the letter together, trying desperately to find out who signed it. It was a pet name—unrecognizable to her; yet the handwriting was familiar.

Carefully she picked through the old coffee grounds and the grapefruit rind to get all the pieces of the card. Written in the same hand as the letter, it was signed, "I love you. Katie."

"My God," she said again as she sank into the chair near the trash bucket. "Is this what I have been reduced to? Searching through the garbage pail? Piecing together a letter from his lover?"

"My God!" she said as she put her hands to her face and began to cry.

That night she broke her engagement with James. Yet, every time she put dried flowers into a trash bucket, she remembered where she had been.

Another fear that sexual addiction can generate in the coaddict is the fear of sexual deprivation which is linked to the faulty core belief that sex is the most important sign of love.

In an addictive relationship great importance is placed on the sexual side of love. Usually this belief is generated from the attitudes and example found in the family of origin.

It could be that procreation held high priority in the family of origin. Parents who do not choose to limit their family size for whatever reason create an environment where sexual reproduction indirectly influences a household for many years.

Procreation may be emphasized in a family where fertility is a problem, also. In an indirect way, an only child who has come after several miscarriages may pick up the values of parents who are excessively concerned with sexual reproduction.

All families differ in their priorities. Some, like the two described, can be excessively concerned with sexual reproduction. Inherently, children notice the priorities of the parents.

Although general family patterns and attitudes have an indirect effect on children's beliefs about sex, the most direct negative influence comes through sexual abuse of children. A child who has been sexually abused, overtly or subtly, may grow up with an exaggerated sense of his or her own sexuality. It is reasonable to believe that growing up in an environment that fosters a high awareness of sexuality will produce children who value their own sexuality and ability to function sexually.

If sex has been important in the family of origin, a threat to sexual security in later life can be frightening and cause fears about the relationship itself. The fear of sexual deprivation can be real for the coaddict who lives with sexual addiction.

The multiple affairs of a sex addict are threatening to the sexual relationship of a couple. The coaddict senses this threat and reacts. The coaddict believes that if the sex life of the couple should fail, the relationship will also fail. That may or may not be true, but the coaddicted spouse responds to the fear of sexual deprivation and to the ultimate loss of the loved one. The fears and the faulty beliefs reinforce and support one another. The cycle of addiction goes on.

The addict may subconsciously promote the idea that the coaddict is not a worthy sexual partner. The coaddict may compare his or her partner with other partners; the addict may find a flaw and reveal it. So subtle is this process that the coaddict may not even suspect the negative inference, or may accept it as true and try to adjust to please the addict.

Sometimes the coaddict may even beg the question in an attempt to offset his or her own fears. The coaddict may be so insecure that he or she needs to know all about the partner's previous sexual experience. Upon investigating this sensitive area, the coaddict may end up feeling "less than." A sexually secure person does not need to find out if he or she is the very best sex partner that lover ever had. It is not important.

77

Ironically, the very thing that the coaddict fears—a cessation of sexual activity—could save the relationship. By rejecting unacceptable behavior and changing the emphasis of the relationship, couples in recovery can save their relationships. Couples do this when coaddicts are honest about the abusiveness of the sexual addiction and the overemphasis on sex in the relationship. They do it when they break through the fear and the faulty beliefs. It is not easy but it is possible. Indirectly, the coaddict might be able to stop the cycle of addiction, effecting change in the addict, and, ultimately, the relationship.

THE COMPULSIVE BEHAVIOR ITSELF

The source of compulsive behavior may be fears derived from faulty beliefs, but whatever the source, it is always negative. It is destructively consuming, emerging from the codependent's inner depths. The behavior is difficult to understand and to control.

Often both the addict and the coaddict get into compulsive behavior—a behavior a person does not want but does anyway—knowing that there may be negative consequences.

Let us look more closely at the behaviors of the coaddict.

Hypervigilance

Most compulsive behavior in a coaddicted person involves a hypervigilant stance. The coaddict doesn't want to miss any detail of the addict's behavior—not even the slightest gesture. Attention is obsessive.

This hypervigilant behavior brings a sense of shame with it. Compulsiveness usually brings accompanying remorse because society tells people to exert willpower and control behavior. But the coaddict feels completely out of control.

The coaddict may feel like a threatened animal, looking to the left, to the right, in front, and in back. The coaddict is anxious, tense, and hypervigilant.

The coaddict's bizarre behavior helps enable the addict. The addict can point a finger at the crazy, preoccupied partner who seems to be chasing windmills in an open field. It is the coaddict who shows signs of the disease. The coaddict is not secure, is not relaxed, and is prone to all kinds of stress-related maladies as the addiction deepens.

Hypervigilance erodes self-respect. In the search for clues of their partner's cheating, coaddicts lie, cheat, and steal. This behavior goes against their values and eventually they lose their sense of dignity.

Lying

Living with someone who lies makes it difficult to remain honest. A kind of duplicitous living goes on. It begins when the addict does not tell the truth about his or her whereabouts, while the coaddict gives the absolute truth. After a time, however, the hypervigilance sets in; the coaddict begins to lie about his or her whereabouts just to test the addict, to set traps, or to throw the addict off. It becomes a sick game. Dishonesty breeds dishonesty.

The addict may drive around to find out if a certain lover is at home or if the spouse is not at home. The addict might visit that neighborhood several times a day or frequent a place where there can be new partners. Likewise, the coaddict may drive by the addict's workplace to see if the addict is there. When the couple meets later that night, neither of them can detail the day honestly.

The addict may leave work early to meet a "friend" at a motel because the addict's spouse would never allow the "friends" to continue their relationship and meet in a more public place. Ultimately, the friends succumb to their surroundings and become sexually involved. The spouse leaves work early to check all of the motels in the area, but misses the one where the addict is meeting the friend. Although the spouse doesn't locate the addict, the spouse knows he or she has not been at work all afternoon.

The addict comes home and senses the spouse's anger. Gingerly asking how the day has been—an innocent question—the coaddict has to lie. "Checking motels" would be unacceptable so "Work was fine," or "I left early to go shopping," is offered. A lie!

Then the coaddict begins interrogation, asking about the day's work. The addict lies and says fine because the afternoon was spent in a motel. The coaddict is suspicious but can't confront because he or she, too, has lied about the workday. Both are faced with the discomfort of dishonesty. Their addiction becomes a vicious cycle of lies.

Many times an entire relationship centers around the infidelities and maneuvers of the addict and the coaddict's search for the truth. The relationship becomes a game as the coaddict becomes a compulsive, hypervigilant spy. It is important to note that not all co-addicted partners resort to this demeaning behavior; however, many do.

In *Back from Betrayal*, Dr. Jennifer Schneider makes it clear that coaddicts bring their own set of problems to a relationship. Usually, coaddicts are codependents before they come to the marriage. As Dr. Schneider aptly puts it, "We are not victims; we volunteer." Coaddicts do not know they are volunteers, but they become willing victims.

The person who volunteers for a codependent situation has already experienced some compulsive behaviors in the family of origin. Early home life may have centered around the parent's addiction. If that is true, that parent probably lied to the child, setting the child up for his or her own pattern of lies.

When an innocent five-year-old boy greets his drunken dad at the door and asks, "Where have you been?" he is not told the truth. Addiction breeds lies because the truth hurts too much. Children and co-addicts who live with lies begin to lie to protect themselves. If the same drunken parent sees toys all over the floor and angrily asks, "Who left these toys here?" the five year old might lie and blame a sister to avoid the anger of the parent. Children of alcoholics begin to lie to save themselves from the consequences of their parent's compulsive behavior. Thus they learn to lie compulsively—almost as if the addict prompted them. If it is OK to lie at five, it is probably OK to lie at fifty unless this habit is corrected somewhere along the way.

Lying is futile and counterproductive because it hides the addiction and wastes enormous energy. When one lie is told, it becomes necessary to tell others.

A relationship built on lies lacks the foundation of trust necessary to keep it healthy. By lying, the liar is set up to get caught and thus may never be taken seriously again. There is no feeling as vacuous, futile, and lonely as not being trusted.

Addictive relationships keep the participants in crisis as they learn to dance around issues of trust. Without trust there are questions. One way to check someone's story is to question that person. A partnership riddled with lies and lack of trust can be gauged by the number of questions that are asked.

Without trust, there are omissions. The only way to avoid the truth and stay out of trouble is to omit essential parts of the story. Stories with parts omitted are distorted. They are lies.

To cover another lie or to seem honest, the addict and the coaddict will often omit essential details for their own safety or the safety of others. Sometimes the omissions are just for effect.

Whatever the reasons, little honest intimate relating can go on in an addictive relationship. Too much time is spent on verbal censuring, cataloging, and classifying information. Lies cheat both partners of the spontaneity necessary for intimacy.

Cheating

In a healthy relationship both partners are involved in activities that enhance their spiritual growth. On a daily basis, they work, play, and honor God with their productive lives. In an unhealthy, coaddictive relationship, the partners are preoccupied with sexual exploits and control of the mate.

The coaddict is cheated out of the normal living pattern: everyday work and play, the daily discipline that honors God. The coaddict cheats self of productivity. The coaddict can become a slave to the addiction: the partner's sexual activities.

The coaddict cheats self of needed energy to complete a mission in life. The coaddict loses spiritual ground and does not do what is most essential for a healthy relationship: promote personal spiritual growth and the spiritual growth of a partner.

Both partners lack a helpmate. One is not behaviorally faithful and the other cannot help spiritually because of lack of trust. It is a catch-22 with no discernible ending.

The sex addict is in search of that one lover who will help dispel the terrible sense of aloneness and inadequacy. Yet that search deprives the addict of the most immediate partner. The addict is cheated as he or she cheats. That is the vicious cycle of addiction.

Stealing

Emotionally, the sex addict never has to level with the partner. Physically, the sex addict can always be satisfied. Spiritually, the sex addict steals the seal and symbol of commitment from the partner (presuming sexual fidelity is promised or understood).

To steal something is to take it away without asking permission. The addict steals from the coaddict; the first thing stolen is the necessity for honest relating.

81

If I can run to a sympathetic and often unobjective self-seeking lover who leads me to believe that I am always right and you are always wrong, I never need to be uncomfortable in relating with you.

If you can run to a sympathetic and often unobjective self-seeking lover who leads you to believe that you are always right and I am always wrong, you never need to be uncomfortable in your relating with me.

An addictive relationship is a pseudo-union without honest relating. The addict and coaddict enable outside forces to steal the honesty right out of their relationship. The fiber of the relationship is given to someone else. The couple becomes disloyal.

The second thing the addict steals is the necessity for honest sexuality. Running to a lover who will take care of the addict's sexual needs means the addict does not have to turn to the coaddict's side of the bed. The addict gives away the sexual experiences that can build and sustain a caring relationship. When a couple is there for each other, their relationship is enhanced. That is union. That is bonding.

Because the coaddict senses someone stealing certain rights, he or she learns to steal also.

The first thing the coaddict steals from the addict is the sense of privacy, an essential human right. Everyone needs privacy. Without it, people feel controlled and manipulated. Yet the addict operates in so much secrecy and so many actions affect the coaddict, that he or she incorrectly assumes the right to invade the addict's private domain. This may include listening in on telephone calls, reading letters, searching through desks and the workplace. Once again, the coaddict becomes a spy to accumulate evidence of infidelity. Compulsive behavior is never attractive.

The coaddict seems to believe such compulsive behavior might change things. By trying to prove the infidelities, the coaddict hopes to gain control of the partner and stop the addiction. Because the obsession is so overwhelming, the coaddict might steal letters, diaries, or journals to get proof of infidelity. In finding the proof, the coaddict confiscates it and hangs onto it. This is theft. No matter how it is rationalized, it is stealing.

Lying, cheating, and stealing are all compulsive activities of sexual addiction and coaddiction. They cause loss of values and dignity for both parties. Once caught in this deceitful web, escape is very difficult.

When I first met my husband, we had an innate sense of trust. We told each other everything and were spontaneous with each other.

We could share anything that came to mind. Our relationship was vital, exciting, and beautiful.

Perhaps I delude myself as I reflect fondly on those early courtship days, but I don't think so. We were like two children discovering each other. We were genuinely excited with every new twist and turn on our course.

Then came the first round of infidelities. That really wounded our relationship. It damaged the spontaneity, that delightful childlikeness. It made it all so different. What I thought was a loving, faithful union was not. What I thought was an honest, open bonding was not. I was betrayed into thinking one way about us when another truth was now evident.

I will never forget the moment I realized it was all an illusion. The lies made it all seem dark and dirty. I hated him for doing such a terrible thing to me and to our relationship. I cried for myself, but most of all I cried for the death of those childlike trusting moments, knowing they were gone forever.

It took a few more years to end, but that night, the night I sobbed, I knew it was really over. Sexual addiction takes the trust out of a relationship and sets it afloat on a sea of doubt. That night was the beginning of many doubts and uncertainties. We never returned to our original selves again. Sexual addictions kill relationships, leaving the partners stunned and broken.

NEGATIVE CONTROLS

In addition to negative behaviors, the addict and coaddict may embrace tactical changes made with the belief that the addiction will go away.

The first may be a geographic cure. When the affairs get too close, too hectic, the addict may suggest a geographic move. The coaddict believes (really believes) that the move will help the relationship. It is appealing because it would seem to take the pressure off both partners. The coaddict hopes it will stop the compulsive behavior of the addict. Many alcoholics use this geographic cure to avoid the consequences of their drinking.

While the couple plans the move, hopes are high and it almost seems like it will work. Soon after the couple settles into the new community, however, the acting out starts all over again. The new residence is just another fertile ground for exploration. The coaddicted partner sinks into despair, realizing the geographic cure did not work. Changing locations doesn't change people. Unless the addiction is squarely addressed, the addict will surely continue the cycle as will the coaddict.

If the sexual addiction has surfaced in courtship, the partners may use the tactic of marriage. The coaddict may believe that a more committed structure like marriage will end sexual promiscuity. The coaddict is convinced that marriage will be the control that makes the addiction go away. When it doesn't and the first affairs surface, the coaddict is devastated to learn about something he or she was fully aware of before the marriage. For most people, marrying someone repeatedly untrue is unthinkable.

A very sad tactic is the mistaken decision to have children. A child, they believe, will fix up their tattered and unhealthy relationship. But bringing a child into a sick union only makes the relationship worse and confuses the issues. Not only will the coaddict be more encumbered with the family but there will be one more reason to preserve the status quo. And if the coaddict is the primary caregiver, it can offer the addict more occasions for acting out sexually.

Negative behaviors—lying, cheating, and stealing—and negative controls such as making changes to exact certain behavior from the addict always seem to produce negative results. These measures are employed only out of desperation. Operating out of despair is precarious.

Buying a house, getting married, or having a baby at the wrong time are misguided strategies that are bound to result in disaster. Once-in-a-lifetime decisions should be planned carefully to avoid poor timing and the inevitable unhappy results.

As the negative consequences of behaviors become evident, the ultimate message conveyed to the coaddict is, *you are not a worthwhile person.* The message diminishes self-esteem to an even lower point.

When self-esteem goes, values are compromised, remorse and despair set in. For the addict, that can mean more compulsive acting out as the search for love and approval become intensified. For the coaddict, it can mean a tighter grip on the addict as fear sets in. Once again, the addictive cycle is set in motion to continue its destructive path.

CHAPTER

SEVEN

Finding Self: The Solution

Grant me the serenity to accept
the things I cannot change,
the courage to change the things I can,
and the wisdom to know
the difference.

In his book, *Stage II Relationships: Love Beyond Addiction* (San Francisco: Harper and Row Publishers, 1987, p. 109), Earnie Larsen repeats one key phrase: "If nothing changes, nothing changes." He goes on to explain that change does not occur by itself for we must do something different in order to produce different results. He concludes that change takes place in three stages: conversion, decision, and program.

So it is with love addiction. Someone has to change. The addict will not change since he or she isn't even aware of the sickness. The coaddict must change.

In the first stage, *conversion, the coaddict recognizes the seriousness of the situation.* He or she has had enough pain and realizes that a loss is imminent. The coaddict is pushed to action and decides to surrender.

Conversion happens in different ways for different people and relationships. Discovering an affair can cause conversion for some. A particularly embarrassing situation or the culmination of several embarrassing situations may cause conversion for others. Whatever it takes, a new determination of the will to make things different emerges.

85

Unfortunately, some relationships are severed before any change takes place. Unless the partners get help they may go into similar addictive situations. Once again, if nothing changes, nothing changes.

Once the conversion experience has happened, once the coaddict has reached a bottom, there is hope for the relationship; there is hope for recovery. Ironically, it is at a most negative point that the situation reverses to become positive again. Until the coaddict recognizes that he or she cannot withstand any more pain without the loss of self, personal integrity, physical health, or the relationship itself, nothing changes.

In the second stage, a *decision* must be made. Things must be different in this primary relationship. Old habits must be broken and new behaviors embraced. In wrestling with a decision, remember these important points.

- Decision making can't be avoided if things are to change.
- Accumulating evidence and then outguessing oneself by rationalization can go on forever.
- Don't consider what others think.
- Nothing is more painful than indecision.
- Do not wait too long or some options may be lost.
- Pain and grief are normal in any decision due to grief for the former place of indecision.
- Changing can't be done alone. A support system is necessary.
- The partner needs to understand any major decision.
- Consider the timing of all decisions.
- Make decisions out of a position of strength rather than weakness.

No one ever said that fighting addiction is easy. No one ever said that disengaging from the addictive cycle can be done without great courage. No one ever said this fight will be totally successful and end in victory. But I suggest that at this point of decision there are no other options except, perhaps, flight.

Flight is an option many have chosen. It always carries a chance of future regrets, yet it is an option. This is a decision one must make in the light of one's own circumstances and conscience.

There is no right or wrong in staying in or leaving a sick relationship. Our relationships can be involved, uninvolved, or on hold. However, a relationship on hold will, at some point, have to move off the mark and the parties move closer or further apart. A decision must be made.

Once a decision is made, honor it or credibility will be lost. The longer the wait, the less effective the coaddict is in working through to a positive conclusion. Timing can be important in decision making.

I remember being so desperate to know when it was the right time to do things. As an adult child of an alcoholic, my decision making was not polished and practiced by the time I reached adult years.

When I was faced with addiction in my marriage, I hesitated, procrastinated, and suffered through my own indecision. It was detrimental to any healthy progress toward recovery. My indecision enabled my addicted loved one to stay within his own addiction.

I was afraid to speak the truth, and he covered up his addiction and continued his affairs. I always felt trapped by the addiction because he would lose his reputation and career if I spoke the truth. I felt forced to live the lie too. Yet I knew that at some time there would be a breaking point.

When I forced the truth out into the open, he offered to go for treatment if I would stand by him. I did not understand that I would have only one such moment and that I needed to seize it. The moment passed, he didn't go into treatment, I stayed, and the addiction returned to its active state. By then, it was too late. I had lost my credibility.

A decision entails commitment to new behaviors. Remember: if nothing changes, nothing changes. This is the new *program.*

When change is taking place in my life, I need to do a great deal of thinking and sharing. I have to decide exactly what negative behaviors are defeating me and what positive behaviors need to be substituted. A good exercise at this point is to list those negative behaviors that need to stop and the positive ones that need to start. Be specific by adding the resulting actions. For example:

Stop: putting the addict first.

Start: being good to myself.

Action: The next time the addict approaches a woman in front of me, I will leave the room.

The program needs to be specific and focused on changing the denial, obsession, and compulsive behavior. Let us look at these areas of dysfunction.

BREAKING DENIAL WITH TRUTH

Denial can be broken with truth, but the coaddict usually can't do this alone. The mind becomes clogged, nonfunctional. Thinking needs to be repaired. Actually, it is as if our minds need to be flushed out, routing the denial from every crevice. That takes much work and knowledge.

The first way to break denial is through education. Learn about the disease of sex and love addiction. Read current books on the subject and absorb it all. Reading is a start in opening up the mind.

If there is a local SAnon, go to it. Ask questions and share experiences with others. This is a disease that is cunning and baffling. A great deal of help is needed to break down denial.

To repair thinking, there is a need to get reality based. Coaddicts find themselves completely out of touch with what is real. What they perceive is a delusion, a sincere delusion. That is addiction. That is denial.

Here are some questions one should answer and perhaps discuss with a trusted counselor.

Preoccupation
Is your partner preoccupied much of the time?
Do you accept unacceptable behavior?
Do you reward inattention with attention?

Ritualized behavior
Are you preoccupied with the way your partner relates to others?
Are you hypervigilant?
Are you overly aware of your partner's patterns of behavior?

Compulsive behaviors
Does your partner seem to fight to preserve the right not to be questioned about his or her whereabouts?
Is that an issue, and do you often feel uneasy about questioning where your partner has been?
Does your partner seem inconsistent in open sharing?
Are you open in your sharing?
Do you lie?
Are there inconsistencies in your partner's behavior?
Are you inconsistent in your behavior?

Does your partner omit certain details in sharing?
Do you omit certain details in your sharing?

Despair
Do you get mixed messages from your partner about love?
Do you give mixed messages to your partner about love?
Do you sense that you might not be "good enough" sexually?
Does this cause you to feel a sense of despair?
Do you see visible signs of despair in your partner?

Hopelessness
Are there mood swings in you and in your partner?
In the addict, do these seem to be emotional hangovers not related
to your relationship?
In you, do they seem to be related to your relationship?

Go over these questions with a qualified person who understands
the whole process of sexual addiction. Without this help, one can remain imprisoned in delusional reality. It may be necessary to seek
treatment at a facility that deals with sexual coaddiction or codependency. The ideal is for both parties to seek treatment at the same
time at a good facility. Three such facilities are Golden Valley
Health Center in Minneapolis, Minnesota; Sierra Tucson in Tucson,
Arizona; and Caron Foundation in Wernersville, Pennsylvania.

BREAKING THE DENIAL
BY FACING YOUR FEELINGS

Impaired emoting keeps a person in denial. If feelings are not validated, then change is not necessary and one can continue to avoid
painful feelings. But facing the truth means emoting honestly, without pretense.

For the coaddict, pretending to feel one way while actually feeling
another way is a normal part of living. ACOAs are prime targets for
addictive relationships because they have grown up hiding their feelings.

Generally, the sex addict looks good to the world and speaks,
touches, and persuades gently. Anyone could be happy with this person. But the addict's multiple affairs are emotionally abusive to the
coaddict. The coaddict can say:

"I don't have the loving relationship that everyone sees. I have a dead one and no one has allowed me to bury it. I am sad. Yet, the world expects me to put on a happy face and pretend that all is fine in my world. I will look happy on the outside but am sad in my 'gut.'"

In order to change, the coaddict must allow the sadness to be where it belongs—on the dead relationship. To break the denial of this addiction, the coaddict may have to go through a grieving process rather than try to deny what is already half dead or dysfunctional. The dead components of the relationship are open communication, honesty, and true love. All of these dead parts need burial. That is sad. The coaddict must accept and face a very sick situation in order to turn to health.

To change, the coaddict must admit the anger rather than let it turn into depression or turn it on others. What is the target of the coaddict's anger? Isn't it the addiction? Isn't it the dysfunctional cycle he or she is in? Isn't it some anger at the self for taking part in the cycle?

Anger will not go away. Anger will eat a person alive from the inside out. Anger that is unbridled destroys people, often the very people the coaddict cares about.

It does no good to be angry at the partners, self, or others. But it does make sense to let the anger out on the addiction itself. Having a program means being honest with anger and using it to create the kind of action that will combat the sexual addiction. Anger can give the courage to refuse to be present in the face of the addict's acting out. This may mean that the politician's wife leaves her public role, an honest public position. That is as it should be. This may mean the wife leaves the restaurant as soon as her husband makes eye contact with other women. That is as it should be. This may mean the wife throws the *Playboy* magazine into the incinerator so the kids won't see it. That is as it should be. Anger can be a catalyst to change if it works in the right direction, if it is honest. Here are some questions that might help a person face real feelings:

Anger
    Are you angry at the way your partner is treating you?
    Are you angry at yourself for the way you are acting?
    Where does the anger go?
    Is it expressed or repressed?

Sadness
When do you feel sad?
Are you grieving a loss of relationship?
How do you express this sadness?

Fear
Are you afraid of losing your lover?
Are you afraid of being abandoned sexually?
Does fear cause you to become immobile?

Joy
What makes you happy?
Are you developing things in your life that provide joyful moments?
Does much of your happiness center around your lover and your sexuality?

When the coaddict hits bottom, a flood of feelings is likely to pour in. For so long, the coaddict has had the tendency to defer or repress those feelings. Now they flood in.

"Betrayed again" is more than an expression, more than a mere phrase. It is translated into anger that borders on rage, and sadness that touches depression.

All the symptoms of this long-standing grief can become powerful emotions. Suddenly, seeing each step of the betrayal or several betrayals and the reality of it produces an ongoing rush of vitriolic, all-consuming feelings.

Hang on to the feelings and be prepared to deal with them. It would not be wise to strike out in anger at this point. It would not be wise to do something rash when experiencing such unreasonable and oftentimes unbearable excesses of emotion.

A member of SAnon wrote this letter to me.

Dear Chris,
Right now I am so angry at Mike that I feel I could do physical harm to him. What is worse is the fact that Mike is so loved and respected by everyone. Being a policeman has made him a respected member of the community. For years he has made me look life a fool. All of our friends and the other guys on the force think that I am the problem. To them, I look like the jealous wife.

It is the betrayal, it is the lack of loyalty to himself, to me, and to the community. How do you fight that?

I feel like a fool. I am furious and I have no place to go. If I tell anyone the truth, he is apt to lose his job. When things became impossible, I left the relationship and our friends were critical of me.

Sometimes I think I should have stayed and told the truth, even if it meant Mike's job. But I didn't and now I am alone and being blamed for the destruction of the marriage. It may be years before Mike gets help and others may be harmed by his addiction. He will just go on.

Most of the anger and sadness that I feel, however, is directed at myself because I am the codependent. I knew Mike had several affairs during our courtship but I believed things would change. I could change things.

In my sickness, I really believed that he would be faithful in marriage. Not only did the infidelities continue but I "became the problem." That makes me angry!

My anger is at myself for putting myself in such a terrible spot. My anger is at the time, energy, and resources that I brought to this union. All were wasted and misused. By trying to gain love, I gave up my self—and the price was too high. I am angry!

BREAKING OBSESSION BY FINDING FREEDOM

Getting free from the obsession of coaddiction involves a conscious effort to break the mental preoccupation with the addict.

Breaking free means really salvaging self from an imposed, personal bondage. This may sound severe but it is not.

Many coaddicts have come to their marriages with an existing problem. The problem is simply that they have dedicated their lives to others to the neglect of self.

The first step in breaking free is to make a conscious effort to stop talking about or "obsessing" over the addict. Let it go, mentally first, and the rest will follow. This can be done in or out of the relationship. It doesn't matter; either way is difficult.

However, as difficult as this is to do, it is essential that the coaddicted partner disengage from constant preoccupation with the addict so that recovery can begin. If the partner is preoccupied with others, the coaddict plays into that addiction by becoming preoccupied with the addict. The focus must shift back to the coaddict and the coaddict's behavior.

Coaddicts do not belong to themselves. They give themselves away. Others rent space in their heads on a regular basis; they are owned.

When the addiction is sexual, breaking the obsession becomes more intricate. When sexual identity—a person's womanhood or manhood—is tied into another person, all perspective is lost.

Breaking the obsession, getting free, can be thwarted by rationalizations and sincere delusions that seem stronger than the desire to get free. Because the coaddict is obsessed by someone else, he or she is controlled by them.

An obvious symptom of coaddiction is the coaddict's need to control the lover's behavior. In reality, the coaddict is emotionally owned—bought and sold—by the addict.

Look at this idea and internalize it. Codependents do not value themselves. They waste their mental time and energy on another.

Coaddicts buy into the idea that they are responsible for the addicts' behavior. If the addict has an affair at the office and loses his or her job, the coaddict suffers and tries to thwart that possibility. The coaddict suggests that the addict get help, takes away the pain, and often hinders the addict from hitting bottom.

In retrospect, I look at my years of living with sexual addiction and am amazed. It is so apparent to me that I felt responsible for every action that my husband engaged in. In so many ways, I shielded him from himself—from his own addiction.

In essence, when I was obsessed about him and made it difficult for him to meet his lovers, I enabled him. When I confronted his girlfriend by going to her husband, I became the problem and he continued to see her secretly.

It was like the wife of the alcoholic throwing the alcohol down the sink in an effort to stop her husband from drinking. The alcoholic simply gets more alcohol. As I got rid of one lover, another one quickly took her place.

One of the reasons it is difficult to live with sexual addiction is because it is an affront to a person's dignity and touches a person at the most intimate level. Many people cannot stand idly by while their partners have sexual relations with others. Yet, it does little good to make an effort to stop the addiction until the addict is ready to quit. Not until the addict feels enough pain and suffers the consequences will he or she be ready to quit.

There are some general rules that the codependent can follow while breaking free from addiction.

Stop bargaining

The coaddict entertains a sincere delusion that if he or she can do more, the addict will stop the unacceptable behavior. All the bargaining in the world will not change the obsession of the addict. In fact, the cessation of the coaddict's bargaining may change the addict more quickly than anything else.

The family parallels an alcoholic home. When the spouse goes to AlAnon and starts to get well, it often happens that the addict stops drinking. When the coaddict bargains with the addict, interest is diverted from the addiction onto the latest bargaining point. An addict will allow the attention to be diverted to anything other than the addiction. If focus is firmly set on the addiction, then the addiction will have to stop. In the case of alcoholism, it is drinking. In the case of sexual addiction, it is acting out sexually.

A coaddict can set up all kinds of bargains in an attempt to control the addict and stop the emotional pain. The coaddict can try to be a better sexual partner, better housekeeper, or a more attractive person. The coaddict can bargain, bargain, bargain until nothing is left.

Stop people pleasing

If a coaddict expresses anger, or frustration, or any other normal emotion, the addict might be displeased. And if the addict is displeased, he or she might go to someone else. So, in an effort to win and keep favor with the addict, the coaddict learns to "people please."

In this never-ending gift-giving situation, the addict takes as much as the coaddict wishes to give away. Most of the time the addict is not looking for these gifts, but the coaddict willingly sacrifices them. The addict gets used to being showered with gifts. Actually, the addict can feel controlled, even bastardized, by such generosity and martyrdom.

A coaddict who loved too much looked back with these reflections.

It is only in looking back that I see how little I valued what I had when I met Jack. We were both in the program and I was well on my way to recovery from alcoholism. Having had nine years of sobriety, I was working on an MSW degree at the university, with the possibility of teaching there some day. I owned my own home, had three-fourths of my retirement paid, and earned over thirty-five thousand dollars a year.

Within a period of three years, I lost forty-six thousand dollars on my property, dropped out of my degree program, took an extremely early retirement, and moved to a state without employment resources.

I did this freely, willingly, without being asked, because it was necessary for my husband to change jobs to avoid the consequences of his sexual addiction. His need became mine and I devalued myself. What took me years to build, I gave away to please a man who could not make a commitment to me.

My reasoning was that if I made a greater commitment, then he would, of course, commit.

Breaking the obsession of sexual addiction means freeing self from the loved one and protecting the self. Left to one's own devices, the coaddict will, in the addictive state, give away all that he or she has.

Listen to the self

Learning to be intuitive, learning to listen to the voice within, is difficult for many people. Perhaps outside forces have controlled us at various times in our lives. Perhaps we lived in an alcoholic home as a child. Perhaps we were victims of incest or emotional abuse.

When the world becomes threatening and overwhelming, there is no time or energy to look within. When there is change and confusion everywhere, it is hard to find a quiet place for listening. Yet, listening is a must in order to hear the messages of the self:

What do you really want?
What do you need for you?
How do you feel?
What are your priorities?
What do your instincts say to you?
What about this relationship?

Listen to yourself. Breaking free from obsession helps the coaddict be more in tune with that inner self, the one that knows the co-addict's wishes, needs, and desires.

Be good to yourself

Being good to yourself is different from being selfish. A selfish person thinks only of self. A person who is good to that self develops it to share with others. This person does not give away possessions but builds resources that inspire and enlighten, prompting others to do the same.

Being good to yourself can be something as simple as indulging in an ice-cream soda or as complex as avoiding a negative force in a loved one. Loving another person does not mean taking part in their negative behavior.

In sexual addiction, the coaddict feels that unacceptable behavior is being done to him or her. The coaddict takes personal offense. Many times the coaddict can conveniently step out of the way and let the addict act out unilaterally.

The wife of a public figure who is sexually addicted often feels helpless to exact change. A member of SAnon in this position shared her thoughts with me:

At the most desperate time of my marriage, I found myself in a terrible position. The multiple affairs of my husband were causing an uneasiness and a general aura of discord that was obvious to anyone who saw us as a couple. It would have been terrible in an ordinary social situation, but my husband was the mayor of a large city.

I felt responsible for his reputation. If I did not show up for a fund-raiser, I would feel guilty. Actually, he would meet his latest women friends at the fund-raiser. I was caught in a no-win situation and it caused me torment. No matter what I did, I seemed wrong.

Unfortunately, it wasn't until much later that I realized my behavior was not connected to my husband's. When I recognized that I never put myself first and was not adept at being good to myself, I began to change. It was slow and awkward at first, but I started to say no.

The first time I said no and refused to go to a public event because of my pain and discomfort at his attention to other women, he went crazy. It was my fault and my problem. I didn't listen to him. I listened to myself and persisted in my refusals. He was forced to attend his events alone and his unacceptable behavior became more and more obvious to others. Soon I was not alone in my awareness of my husband's inappropriate attention to women. Finally, his advisors discreetly took him aside and suggested a change in his behavior. Shortly after that, my husband sought treatment for sexual addiction.

Develop resources

You are a child of God with many gifts. You are not attached to your loved one in a dependent way. You are alone, yet you are of God and with God.

Ultimately, getting free means moving away from the addict and coupling with a higher power. Being a child of God gives the power one needs to quell the fear, to move away, to develop resources.

Without God's help, addiction can destroy. With God's help, it can be conquered. However, it takes an active decision, much prayer, and meditation to move off the mark and closer to God.

BREAKING COMPULSIVE BEHAVIOR WITH DISCIPLINE

In *Stage II Relationships: Love Beyond Addiction,* Earnie Larson claims that "no relationship can be healthier than the people involved in it" (p. 20). He reiterates that the first commitment is to personal growth. When the coaddict lacks the discipline to stop his or her compulsive behavior, he or she adds to the addiction of the partner.

As discussed in chapter six, the coaddict becomes involved in setting elaborate traps to catch the addict cheating. Then the coaddict lies to cover up the traps, cheating himself or herself of time, energy, and peace of mind, trying to change the addict with controlling behaviors. These behaviors are negative and self-defeating; they cause a loss of dignity and self-respect. They are the reasons for the despair and remorse. They are cyclic and futile and need to be stopped if recovery is to take place.

A coaddict can rationalize compulsive behaviors away because they seem less destructive than the sexual acting out of the love addict. But in reality, these compulsive behaviors are just as destructive as the behavior of the addict. In some ways they are worse because they are carried out in a self-righteous way or with moral overtones.

It is true that the sex addict is involved in behavior which is hurt-

97

ful to the coaddict. But it is also true that the addict is dealing with a sickness. So is the coaddict. The addict becomes addicted to the acting out and the coaddict becomes addicted to the addict. The dependence of the addict on love and sex for self-worth is no more an issue than the dependence of the coaddict on the addict for love and sex.

To change this compulsive behavior, the coaddict needs to get help against the negative forces that cause its continuation. Help can take many forms. It may mean therapy to discuss the root of the coaddict's addiction. The coaddict may need to examine the way he or she views sex. Is there a history of incest in the family? The child of an alcoholic may need to look at ACOA issues such as the fear of abandonment. The coaddict might need a group like COSA (Codependents of Sex Addicts) for the families of sex addicts.

Compulsive behavior is broken with discipline. Remember: If nothing changes, nothing changes.

There are no rights or wrongs in these decisions; each coaddict is different. For example, an incest victim usually needs intensive psychotherapy while others can get the help they need at a COSA meeting. Wherever one turns, it is important to seek outside help. Caring persons can monitor behavior and give warnings when negative patterns return.

Twelve-step programs have an expression about codependence. It says, "Listen to those gut level reactions!" When I am about to enter into a cycle of compulsive behavior, my body warns me. I get a dull pain in the pit of my stomach as if someone is kicking me there. That is the signal. Something instinctive is happening. There is strong emotion—fear, terror, anger. I feel threatened.

Now I understand that these feelings are warning signs. Usually I try to recognize exactly what I am feeling and find some way to clarify the situation. Instinctive reactions say a great deal about a person. These signals should be faced, talked out, not repressed.

In my experience, compulsive behavior can start right after I sense this dull pain. I may start to control so that the pain won't get any worse. Rather than act offensively, I retreat and become defensive. I try to control that person so that he or she won't do whatever it is that I fear. Rather than ask for an explanation or confront the person, I retreat, maneuver, and sabotage any honest relating. That dishonesty can make the situation worse—and usually does.

Take heed of those gut level reactions. They may signal compulsive reactions. Stop, listen, and take control of self at that point. Go offensive immediately!

First discipline: letting go of hypervigilance

Letting go is a loving form of detachment. It does not mean hiding from what is happening to a loved one. But it does mean detaching emotionally from the symptoms of the disease that troubles the addict. In the simplest terms, "mind your own business."

If a loved one is acting out sexually, it is difficult not to be hypervigilant. The coaddict watches everyone, trying to catch the addict in an unfaithful act. Watching the addict actually gives him or her more excuses for not owning the behavior. The addict rationalizes that the coaddict's hypervigilance is the reason for acting out. Remove the scrutiny and the addict has to own his or her behavior.

It is difficult to let go of situations that are troublesome because the addict purposely seeks to set up those situations. Like the alcoholic who creates a crisis, the love addict sets up encounters with other people.

If recovery is to take place, it is essential to let go. Some coaddicts can't do this in the framework of the marriage and they need time away to detach. However, it is possible to remain in the relationship and stop the hypervigilance. Here are some rules.

- Don't keep track of the addict's whereabouts.
- If the addict is not in recovery, allow the freedom to come to his or her own decision about the disease unless to do so would seriously harm you. (With the problem of AIDS today, it may be necessary to protect yourself by refusing to be sexually involved until your partner gets treatment.)
- Say no to situations that are physically or emotionally dangerous to you, even if it means detaching from mutual social situations.
- Be clear about the reason you are removing yourself from unacceptable situations.
- Take control of your own life and allow the addict to take control of his or hers.

Second discipline: stop keeping secrets, stop lying

Becoming honest in a dishonest relationship is not easy. It is much easier to rationalize the situation and deny the severity of the dysfunction. It is much easier to lie and preserve the illusion of a loving relationship.

Most people want to be in a loving relationship, but in sexual addiction the coaddicted partner is willing to compromise values and keep secrets rather than accept the possibility of a failed relationship. Where there are secrets, there is also trouble.

A person is only as free as the number of secrets one carries. Secrets are heavy and weigh people down. Refusing to keep secrets, refusing to lie to self and others, make recovery impossible.

Third discipline: stop cheating yourself and others

Discipline involves changes that are not always easy to carry out. Ultimately, the coaddict has to stop cheating self and others.

Shifting focus from the addict to the self, the coaddict has made the first step in recovery. Now it is time to change behaviors. It is not easy at first. Habitual, negative behaviors are so comfortable. To remain focused on the lover is so native that it seems painful to center on self.

Look at a given behavior; for instance, stopping by the office to check on a partner or calling the addict who is late coming home. Both of these behaviors cheat the coaddict of precious time and energy. These need to be changed.

The only way to change compulsive behavior is to make a list of negative behaviors. Then stop doing those things even though you don't want to stop. It takes a firm commitment to stop compulsive, habitual actions, but it can be done.

- Decide which behaviors need to be avoided.
- Have a plan for confronting these behaviors.
- Tell a counselor or sponsor about your plan.
- Use self-talk and, when tempted, call your sponsor.
- Stick to your plan even when you don't want to.
- Ask God for needed help.

Fourth discipline: setting limits

Discipline does not mean merely doing nothing or avoiding certain negative behaviors. It can mean going on the offensive and imposing some positive controls.

At ACOA meetings there is a saying, "You didn't cause it, you can't control it, and you can't cure it, but you can cope with it." In other words, it is possible to control a response to any addiction. I the person is truly powerless over the addiction, let it go to God.

For some coaddicts, the idea of letting go sounds inviting and frightening at the same time. A natural tendency says "There, the burden is lifted and I never have to deal with this terrible problem again." On the other hand, letting go is tantamount to no control at all and that can be frightening.

These are extremes: rigid control or reckless letting go. These however, are not the only two choices. There is a third, a middle ground of moderate control. In this middle ground, the spouse picks and chooses which situations to deal with and when. So there is a partial letting go for proper balance.

One of the key issues in dealing with any addiction is the ne cessity of prudent, thoughtful decision making. It is easy to get into all or nothing thinking when put in a tight spot. SLOW DOWN Check options carefully and GET HELP in sorting things out. Reacl out to others, then MAKE SOME WISE DECISIONS.

Several types of positive controls can be used inside and outside the relationship. However, most couples need the guidance and sup port of others to establish and monitor these controls.

No relationship can run helter-skelter without limitations. The sex addict leads the coaddict to believe that it can. The sex addict balk at any constraints on his or her activities. The addict will insist that the coaddict is possessive and jealous.

Making contracts that define acceptable and unacceptable be haviors, and assigning consequences, are a good method to use in re covery. A counselor competent in sexual addiction should monito and maintain these contracts or they may fail.

Contracts that the coaddict draws up hastily in frustrated anxiety are practically useless. They don't have the force of those that ai outsider witnesses. Unfortunately, contracts are much like an al coholic's pledge never to drink again. In a tight spot, it is easy to mouth words. It is more difficult living them. Addiction is cunning baffling, and insidious. If it were easy to arrest, there would be no treatment centers.

Getting help through proper counseling or treatment centers is es sential for couples in recovery. The help must be timely and con sistent. Many marriages have failed because no help was sought

Breaking up does not solve the problem; it simply sends the addict and coaddict out to find a similar situation. If nothing changes, nothing changes.

A good counselor can determine the need for treatment. Treatment centers specifically for sexual addiction are few, but more are opening. With an intervention tactic, an addict may be urged into treatment.

Like alcoholism, treatment of sexual addiction in a hospital setting is more effective if the patient will cooperate. Denial is often broken more quickly in such a setting. Recovery will be progressive just as the disease of addiction was progressive.

Positive controls include support groups, counseling, intervention, and treatment. The more help, the better. As the public becomes more aware and understanding of this addiction, those who suffer from the disease will find more help is available.

EIGHT

A Healthy Relationship

How are loving relationships created? What are they made of? In dysfunctional families, relationships are a puzzle. Members tend to be incapable of relating in a positive way with others.

Perhaps the only way to find some semblance of order in intimate relationships is to look at true dysfunctional relationships and work for exactly the opposite. For those who have already learned the skills of relating, this is an unnecessary exercise; to the addict or co-addict, it is a requirement.

Let us list what constitutes a healthy relationship. Truth is needed to replace denial in the dysfunctional relationship. Trust is needed where there is distrust. Freedom is needed where there is obsession. Discipline is needed where there is compulsive behavior. Tolerance is needed where there is intolerance. And finally, it all takes time, energy, and constant maintenance.

The addict or the coaddict revamping his or her view of personal relationships has taken on a mammoth but worthwhile task. It is good to embark on this venture and try to relate in a healthy way. Otherwise either or both partners will be doomed to feelings of frustration, unhappiness, and a sense of isolation.

DENIAL VERSUS TRUTH

In previous chapters, we learned that denial generates secrecy—and secrecy breeds shame.

A relationship based on shame is always second rate. Who wants anything second rate, especially in an intimate, primary relationship?

A relationship is like a living organism; it needs to be kept in good health. One sure way to insure a healthy, functioning relationship is to tell the truth.

Does that mean never shielding a loved one from a damaging piece of information? No. But it means telling the truth if the relationship will suffer without it.

Secret, cancerous spots on a relationship won't go away. They grow and spread. For example, denying an affair will not cure the damage it does. Likewise, bisexual activity can't be hidden; there is harm and danger in the activity. Dishonesty never works.

Denial is about lying to self and others, pretending that an addiction ignored will disappear. Denial means pretending that relationships are OK when they are not. Lies are nothing but pretending.

Truth is the first step to romance. The coaddict might think it's more romantic to paint a rosy picture, to keep the status quo, or to maintain a confluent state where no one will get angry. Not so. Being pleasant is not the most practical avenue to romance.

Truth is the bedrock of a relationship. Denial covers up serious flaws in the foundation of the relationship. Sooner or later, when an untruth is revealed, the foundation will crack. When that happens, the relationship is in shambles. Repairing a cracked foundation is much harder than living with the rigors of honesty.

For any couple seeking a healthy relationship, honesty must carry over to feelings as well as opinions. Feelings need honest expression. That does not mean abusing a loved one with a constant barrage of negative feelings. It does mean letting the partner know about feelings that affect the relationship.

It is obvious that I can't deal with you unless you let me know honestly how you feel. Nor can you ever hope to understand and love me if I shield my feelings from you. If you don't tell me how you feel, I can never understand your needs and participate in helping you get those needs met.

In a healthy and honest relationship, both lovers have their needs met. Negotiation and compromise are a part of the bargaining resources of the relationship, and these bear fruit for both parties.

It takes honesty to express a need for a little affirmation, attention, sex, money, space—any number of things. It takes healthy self-esteem to know people have the right to ask for special favors. It takes

a great deal of love to return those favors. It demands "give and take."
Risk is involved when one honestly expresses the need for something. The risk comes in putting self on the line and being vulnerable. It means taking a chance that a loved one might refuse your request. For anyone terrified of abandonment, that can mean rejection. Rejection is not a comfortable state for anyone traumatized by dysfunctional parents who were not there for them.

Actually, some codependent persons come to believe they do not have needs. It is better to defer every need rather than be turned away and suffer pain and shame again. Neglected children may have to work diligently to reprogram their adult thinking just to be honest about their needs.

Without honesty, there is no hope for a healthy relationship. Melody Beattie puts this so powerfully in *Beyond Codependency:*

> We can wait until the sky turns purple, but we won't be able to get close to or be intimate with someone who's actively addicted, someone who we believe is lying to us, or someone who we fear might verbally, physically, or emotionally injure us.
>
> Someone abusing, lying, or acting out his or her addiction isn't capable at the moment of the honesty and surrender, acceptance, self-responsibility, disclosure, and exposure necessary for intimacy and closeness. These people aren't present for themselves and won't be present for the relationship. (San Francisco: Harper and Row, 1989)

When there is little honesty in words, expression of feelings, and definition of needs, there is little trust between the partners. When there is little trust, the relationship stagnates and cannot reach its potential. It might escalate to highs in ego enhancement and partial needs fulfillment, but it will rarely reach the higher levels of spiritual growth.

As with so many things in life, a good relationship demands an integral unity, a certain substantive blending that makes for healthy functioning. If truth is not present between lovers, trust cannot follow. Similarly, if trust is not present, there will be little freedom.

TRUST VERSUS DISTRUST

The second essential ingredient in a healthy relationship is trust. The ability to trust creates the climate for intimacy.

How can I let myself fully love you if I can't be sure you are trustworthy? No one gives self to another in an atmosphere of fear and distrust.

For the coaddict living with constant lies and betrayal, there is no hope for growth in the relationship. As soon as the addict and coaddict begin to establish a sense of commitment, that bond is broken. And with it goes trust. It takes time to reach intimacy; it takes trust to build intimacy. Sexual addiction does not foster the consistency necessary to relate intimately.

Couples need to build a climate for intimacy, a climate that includes risk taking, disclosure of feelings, presentation of needs, and setting of boundaries. That climate must be a safe one.

A person can't venture forth, vulnerable to a lover, when he or she is afraid of censure, ridicule, or betrayal. A person can't really give intimately if he or she is not sure that what is given will be respected and not misrepresented.

In sexual addiction the coaddict never really knows where he or she stands because of the lack of commitment. How can the coaddict feel safe at any level of trust if this deeply personal one—sexual intimacy—is in question?

An important task for any couple in a healthy relationship is to protect and nurture their relational environment. Too often couples neglect the environment in which their relationship develops. It is like trying to plant a garden on barren soil—a hopeless task.

Trust is the ingredient that makes the soil fertile. It has to be used liberally at some times and sparingly at others. Sometimes it is wise to trust others and sometimes it is not wise. Sometimes it is wise to trust ourselves and sometimes it is not wise.

When children are told repeatedly that obvious danger is unreal, they eventually learn they have been lied to. Experiencing the danger parents said did not exist, the children become confused. Their original instincts were correct. They soon come to distrust others and even their own perceptions of danger.

Children of alcoholics deal with parents controlled by a very untrustworthy disease. Addiction causes all kinds of dangerous situations, yet children attempt to trust the parent. Overtrusting becomes a major problem. They can repeat this pattern in adult life.

Codependents are not good at listening to themselves in times of danger. They believe the world is safe when it isn't or unsafe when it is. One of the most discouraging aspects of this is the proclivity for unhealthy relationships. Codependents repeatedly will rush into relationships with untrustworthy persons.

Codependent persons are prone to gravitate to the past. They marry into addiction because it is familiar. Trusting the untrustworthy comes easy to codependents since they lived this way with parents. How can the coaddict learn to trust in a healthy way?

Some trust until they are betrayed. On the other hand some do not trust at all because they expect betrayal. These two positions are extremes. Building trust in a reasonable manner lies somewhere in between. An adult relationship needs the middle ground—a slow and often risky process. The natural tendency to distrust has to be challenged; the tendency to overtrust has to be checked. Only then can the adult child or codependent begin to build a reasonable trust level.

Testing is the key. Bit by bit, people check out the honesty and trustworthiness of others. They risk and assess the results, then risk again until they can fully trust. Trust is earned, not permanently withheld or freely given. It takes much time, but mature love can develop only in the presence of trust. Four qualities indicate that trust is authentic.

The first is *reliability*. Can the person be relied on? Does he or she let others down? Does the person keep his or her word? Is the person loyal? Is the person there for others in need?

The second quality is *openness*. Are there secrets surrounding a partner? Why? Secrets usually mean lies. Deliberate holding back on information is a secret and can be as damaging as an open lie. Secrets should signal the untrustworthiness of an individual.

The third quality is *acceptance*. Does this person accept differences in others? When this sense of being accepted is missing, something is clearly out of kilter and trust is not warranted.

The final quality is *congruence*. Congruence means that the person's actions match words. Quite often persons are dishonest with themselves—not congruent in word and action.

Honest persons own their inconsistencies and speak about them. Incongruence can mean deception of self or lying. The trustworthiness of such persons is questionable.

These four qualities are sorely needed to fortify the foundation of an intimate relationship. Test for reliability, openness, acceptance, and congruence. If these qualities are present, then slowly offer parts of self. If these are handled in a responsible way, offer a little more. It's as simple as that; it's as risky as that.

Trust builds healthy relationships and produces results. The individuals experience oneness and separateness in the same relationship. They develop and grow. They ask for what they want. They give and receive. They accept each other. They develop high self-esteem. Being alone is not threatening; being committed is natural; expressing feeling is spontaneous; caring with detachment is common. Partners who trust affirm the equality of the other and honor the personal power of self and others. Trust does it all; it is the foundation for all healthy relationships.

One sure way to develop trust is to trust God. Asking God for help and wisdom in the process of building trust is necessary for everyone. It cannot be done alone. Trust that God will be the guide to a spiritual union with others. When a person reaches a trust level with God, all other relationships seem to take care of themselves.

OBSESSION VERSUS FREEDOM

The trust that bonds a healthy relationship allows the partners to be free because they are not obsessed with controlling each other. They can become obsessed in a productive way with work, family, a special hobby. But they need not be totally dependent upon the time and attention of each other.

Patrick Carnes speaks of this lack of freedom in his description of the coaddict as one who holds on too tight. Out of intensity, obsession, and the need to be in control, the coaddict "...won't let go, and so they imprison themselves within the addictive process. Only through a complete acknowledgment of their own powerlessness... will the coaddict find peace."

Obsession with a partner usually indicates imbalance in the relationship. One or both partners may not be strong enough to stand on their own. With this excessive need for each other, they become codependent. One partner may need to need someone, like the sex addict. The other partner may need to be needed. Whatever the situation, overdependence upon another indicates a lack of freedom.

Addiction always indicates this dependency and imbalance. In sexual addiction, the addict seems annoyed with the coaddict's overattention but, without it, could not function in the addiction. What is, is not always as it seems.

Obsession with any partner in any relationship is a sure sign of an unhealthy relationship.

Why do I have to cling to you so tenaciously? What is it you have that I need? Why can't I find that in myself, in others, in recreation, in career, in children, in community projects, in life? What is it that makes me hold you so tight? Am I so afraid you might go away?

Do you identify me as your sexual partner, as your husband or wife, as an extension of you? Why can't I let go and still be whole? Perhaps I see part of myself in you. Perhaps my boundaries have meshed with yours and I have lost who I am. Perhaps in taking your freedom I have lost mine!

A healthy relationship is never plagued by the question about who is whom. I am me and you are you! You do not ask me to be you nor do I ask you to be me. We can disagree, be angry, or be sad without violating each other's precious identity.

A free-flowing energy is present. This energy allows for less rigid rules and consequently, less tension. There is trust and there is freedom.

An obsessive relationship has clear symptoms of restriction. Listen carefully to one or the other partner to hear repeated conversational patterns that make reference to the lover or the relationship. One or both partners are obsessed. They are the most important thing in the world to each other and the whole world knows it.

A healthy relationship is marked by a balance in the conversational pattern. It changes from politics, to sports, to career, but never dwells on one person and one relationship. It is free and moves about from one point to another.

Unhealthy relationships involve people pleasing and inordinate sacrifices. Sometimes one partner seems willing to give up everything for the lover, consumed by the other to the point of self-destruction. This is not love; it is bondage.

In a healthy relationship power is balanced. No one is asked to carry an unbalanced load. There is compromise, not unreasonable sacrifice.

Bargaining is a mark of conditional love. "I will give you this if you love me!" Viable relationships, on the other hand, are nurtured by negotiations and unconditional love.

Individuals must give up something to be in a relationship. Negotiation requires time and energy, but it is vital. If negotiations do not take place, selfishness and resentment rule. Relationships should not be places where one person bargains away everything he or she is and has—just to be loved.

109

Sex can be overemphasized in an unhealthy relationship. It can become a bargaining chip instead of an expression of love. Sexual acts should be given in freedom with no fear of reprisal or retribution. In sexual addiction, however, the coaddict will agree to unacceptable sexual behavior out of fear of losing the lover.

Obsession usually indicates the presence of low self-esteem. The coaddict thinks less of self as personal identity is surrendered to the partner. The addict thinks less of self for taking too much from the partner. No one needs to lose in a relationship where self-esteem is high. Partners have the confidence of being enough without taking or giving too much time or energy to another.

No boundaries are set in a dysfunctional relationship. Everything has a purposeful ambiguity. Although the absence of boundaries suggests a freer relationship, lack of direction causes confusion rather than freedom. Knowing what is expected enables a person to move about freely and do just what is necessary. If the person does not know the rules—who you are and who I am, where you begin and where I end, confusion ensues. Confusion inhibits the free flow of energy within a relationship.

Boundaries create two distinct beings. One does not bump into the other; both move freely in space. The irony here is that restrictions actually help to create free movement. It is like the meshing of gears which are drawn and move only because they have clear-cut lines. People and relationships are the same, working best with two healthy, self-contained humans.

In dysfunctional relationships, behaviors are motivated by a need to control. The gears don't work on their own; the partners need to push each other to get things done. Controlling behaviors are not easy to interpret, they do not feel safe, nor are they easy to live with. Noncontrolling behaviors are the sign of a functioning relationship. They indicate that the partners have enough health to cope with life on their own terms without needing to exact certain behaviors from others.

When obsession enters a love affair, reality is distorted. An observer will hear rationalizations as the partners attempt to present a positive picture to others: "We are so very close." "There has never been anyone in my life like…." "I will die without his love."

Obsessing persons believe their rationalizations and delusions. Obsessions, however, are not reasonable. They cripple the thinking of codependent persons.

To be free, a relationship must be reality-based. It should be anchored in the reality of the moment. No one should ever feel he or she will die without a partner. If this is the case, too much of self has been given away in the relationship.

Because obsessions are not reasonable, it follows that they promote unreasonable, compulsive behaviors. It takes enormous personal discipline to break through an obsessive situation and keep a healthy relationship from slipping away into an obsessive one.

COMPULSIVE BEHAVIOR VERSUS DISCIPLINE

Compulsive behavior creates a certain unmanageability in the lives of the couple. Repeated negative behaviors bring about negative consequences and unmanageable situations.

I am not in control if I watch every move my partner makes; I am not in control if I feel the need to please people at my own expense. I am not in control if wrong motives determine my actions. Rather, I am behaving compulsively.

Much of the energy that could be channeled into personal accomplishments is wasted in sexual coaddiction. It is obvious that spending time searching through someone's belongings is useless and degrading. Driving by someone's house to check their activity is time consuming. These behaviors represent a compulsion to control the sexual behaviors of the addict.

If the addict can't control them, does the coaddict think he or she can? It takes discipline to mind one's own business. This direct kind of thinking says, "I am not in charge of your behavior; I am in charge of mine." Members of SAnon and AlAnon speak of detachment from the addicted person. It is not an easy task. It requires rigorous discipline.

When I finally made the decision to stop acting compulsively, I became very direct with myself. I had to restrain myself from acting in certain ways. I had denied that it was unseemly to engage in hypervigilant behaviors; therefore as I recovered, the reality of my behavior struck me. I wondered how, if I had any self-esteem, I could possibly have engaged in those demeaning acts.

As my self-esteem grew, these compulsive behaviors became more and more repulsive to me. Something inside said, "You are too good for this." Finally, I was able to exert the will necessary to break into the compulsive behavior and stop it. It took a great deal of self-

111

talk and prayer in those early times of decision.

Rationalizations became blatantly obvious. I could no longer delude myself by self-justifying thoughts such as I have a right to act that way. Don't I have good reason to be suspicious? Don't I have the right to protect myself from hurt and rejection? Don't I have the right to try to control the actions of someone else? I finally realized I did not have these rights. I was using these thoughts to justify my own negative behaviors.

Once awareness comes to the coaddict, it is a matter of exerting self-discipline. Where should all this energy be placed? The coaddict must come back to self, to spiritual growth.

Twelve-step programs have a saying that exemplifies how personal discipline enters into the early days of recovery. It is said that individuals can "act their way into good thinking." What seems right and familiar to a coaddict is probably not right. This is overcome by applying cognitive behavior, controlled by reason, in place of compulsive behavior, a merely reactive emotional response.

In any addiction-based relationship, it takes discipline to focus on the best interests of the self. Like substance abuse, it requires a withdrawal period. Behaviors formerly accepted through rationalizations and denial have to be changed.

Here are some examples of unacceptable behaviors.

- Lying about anything for any reason.
- Keeping secrets and hiding the truth.
- Cheating yourself out of time and energy.
- Giving up important things to retain the love of a partner.
- Not attending to your own friends and family.
- Attacking others; allowing yourself to be attacked.
- Not setting or accomplishing goals.
- Not focusing on yourself; concentrating on the other.
- Not confronting; always giving in.
- Not setting boundaries; staying enmeshed.

The discipline of recovery from compulsive behaviors lies in the ability of the recovering person to seize the focus. This is not a selfish act; it is an act of survival.

Codependency in relationships is dangerous, damaging, and debilitating. Codependency can make a person very sick and can even destroy. There is no other choice, then, but to pull the focus back to self. How is this done?

The first rule to becoming more disciplined is to listen to yourself. It takes strength and courage to listen to what you hear inside, to pay attention to the voice that knows what is best for you. It takes a secure self to stand up against others who would have their wishes fulfilled while yours are neglected. Hear the spiritual part of you that says this behavior is demeaning, that this situation does not feel right.

Secondly, it takes deliberate concentration to be good to yourself. When there are so many outside forces pulling you away from your own center, it is not easy to think of yourself, but this is essential to self-esteem.

If I allow you to take up my time and to deplete my energy, I will not think highly of myself. No matter who you are or what your priorities are, I need to say no to you sometimes and favor myself. It may mean confrontation and you might become angry, but if I am truly in tune with myself, I will be good to myself.

It takes a purposeful sense of determined concentration to develop personal resources. Accomplished people did not get that way by being compulsively undisciplined or by living unmanageable lives. A structured plan is needed to meet goals. A sense of resolve is needed to implement those goals. Being your own person is hard work.

Recovery from codependency allows a new person to emerge. This new person needs new rules and the discipline to stick by those rules. Certain behaviors are unacceptable. Self-inflicted pain is unacceptable. Being a martyr is unacceptable. Wasting time is unacceptable. There are no grievances, only compromises. It is forgiveness, not control. It means not playing God but being more like a child of God.

If I am empty, if I lack love for self, I will need you more. This void can cause an urgent hunger which will dominate our relationship. I need to attend to myself; I need to love myself first.

Ironically, looking to a higher power to help fill this void will relieve the urgent hunger for human love. As faith in God grows, the need for human affirmation is lessened. By working to develop a conscious contact with a higher power I can learn to center upon something other than my partner. Then strength comes from within rather than without. The obsession lifts.

As the obsession lifts and faith grows, I experience the freedom of my own autonomy. That is a wonderful place to be.

TOLERANCE VERSUS INTOLERANCE

When addiction is present in a relationship, intolerance and self-righteousness are there too. The classic example is the alcoholic husband who drinks to excess and the coalcoholic wife who diminishes her own faults by pointing to the excesses of her husband. So it is with the codependent married to a sex addict; the coaddict excuses his or her lack of attention to the children by looking to the behavior of the spouse.

In these unbalanced relationships, the payoff consists in looking at the sins of the other and playing victim. The coaddict's intolerance of the addict enables the coaddict to keep the focus on the addict and away from self. If the coaddict looks closely at self, the problem of codependence will come to the surface.

Most of the coaddict's compulsive behavior shows a measure of intolerance. There is something egotistical about the actions of the coaddict in pursuing the addict, checking every move. These behaviors smack of an attitude that says, "I am better than you. I cannot tolerate you." In truth, codependency is a sickness itself. It is as deadly as the sexual addiction. The addict lusts for many while the coaddict lusts for control over the sexual activities of the addict. Both are dealing with addiction.

A healthy relationship has a sense of dignity which implies a tolerance of the other partner. No one is perfect; everyone needs tolerance for personal weaknesses. In order to maintain a sense of dignity, people need to forgive one another.

Personal dignity used in this sense does not mean accepting unacceptable behavior It simply means acknowledging the God-given dignity that comes with being a child of God.

This is not to say that a loving couple stays in their relationship and simply tolerates each other. Understanding and respect should inform every communication and transaction within that relationship. Isn't that what unconditional love is all about? Unconditional love does not mean accepting abuse, but rather allowing others to be in the space where they are. No one can grow spiritually if they are intolerant.

Authentic love is unconditional. Anger, suffering, or disruption in a relationship are hidden conditions. Usually, it is difficult to see

114

one's own hidden demands but very easy to see the hidden demands of others. Consequently, in a free and open relationship, individuals need to be tolerant enough to understand that they have no right to make their hidden demands.

In sexual addiction, the coaddict demands fidelity. It is assumed that the addict is capable only of infidelity. This implied intolerance and demand for performance do not work well in any relationship.

But what about defending self? Must a person stand idly by and be abused? In any addiction, compulsiveness and an unmanageable condition surface. The coaddict takes offense, thinking the addict is victimizing him or her. In fact, the coaddict is not a special target. An addict will victimize anyone who agrees to it.

The answer does not lie in defense but in defenselessness. In defense, the partner feels attacked and the conflict escalates. In defenselessness, safety and love are given opportunity to resurge.

That does not mean the unacceptable behavior is encouraged. Those who truly love and respect self will neither fight nor give in and withdraw but will deal forthrightly and lovingly with others as equals. Isn't it better for the coaddict to abstain from any sexual contact until the addict seeks help, rather than to leave the relationship? Sometimes the simplest, most honest answers are best.

Much can be said about being an active chooser, moving positively toward a goal rather than reacting to a presumed negative response from one's partner.

As the victim, a coaddict is intolerant in assuming the other means to be harmful. In addiction, there may be little harm intended, but the symptoms of the disease produce harm.

It is important to think of giving and receiving as linked. Giving love generates love in return. Perhaps one of the most difficult things for an active addict to accept is the love and care of a partner who maintains personal dignity and self-esteem.

It is wise to look more closely at a blow received. What contributed to it? Often a blow struck against the coaddict is merely the addict striking back. The question one must ask is "What have I done to contribute to this?" not "What can I do to get even?"

Sometimes we attack subtly, and without our own conscious awareness. For example, walking on eggs around a partner implies that the partner is to be feared or avoided.

Feeling hurt or angry, fearful or pitiful, superior or inferior is a signal to look more closely at the way you are cocreating this situa-

115

tion or subtly attacking your partner. If you are not cocreating a difficulty, you might see someone's attack as a cry for love. Respond by giving love, not by holding back or withdrawing.

Here are some tactics:

- Make a special effort to tap into even the brief moments of warmth and tenderness. Share them.
- Express trivial discomforts. Be honest before they grow into barriers that are harmful in the relationship.
- Every judgment you make is really about yourself. If you are annoyed by the other's behavior, acknowledge your need to forgive that tendency in yourself.
- If you do not perceive the other's shortcomings in yourself, consider that you may be overcompensating in the other direction.
- Tend to your needs. Every time you sacrifice and accommodate your partner's will while ignoring your own, you put space between you and your partner.
- Do not play martyr. Sacrifice breeds resentment and creates obligations that will come due later.
- Be straightforward. You can openly attain what you want without demanding it. Freely permit your partner to say no without coercion.
- Learn to say no to your partner as appropriate.
- Learn to say yes and make agreements that satisfy both of you—agreements that require no sacrifice and both partners are willing to live up to.
- Open your heart to love by silently asking forgiveness for sitting in judgment of your partner's behavior.
- Understand that two emotions govern relationships: love and fear. Every choice you make, every thought you have, every movement you make moves you toward either love or fear.
- Stay out of the past and out of the future. Live in the present moment.
- Teach peace, love, freedom, and joy. Don't resort to conflict, suffering, bondage, and pain. You will learn what you teach.
- Be real. Look to the love and peace that is within you.
- Accept yourself exactly as you are—a child of God. Accept others in the same way. God makes no distinctions.

Once a relationship becomes viable, it demands commitment.

There are places to go and things to do together. Mutual interests are cohesive agents in the making of relationships, but they take time and energy. Without them, a couple can drift apart.

The expenditure of time and energy should remain balanced between partners in a healthy relationship. Although it can never be 50/50 all of the time, such equilibrium is a worthwhile goal. Of course, in a crisis the burden can shift considerably to one partner. However, relationships can't exist with that kind of imbalance from day to day. Love takes energy because it is an action—a decision—not a feeling. Check your energy output and see where it is going.

The final ingredient for a wholesome relationship is maintenance. No one can possibly be truthful, trusting, disciplined, tolerant, and free from compulsive behaviors all of the time. Therefore, relationships need to be checked periodically. Ask some difficult questions and listen to the answers. When the question or answer eludes, seek professional help.

No one would junk a Mercedes-Benz because the engine sputters and won't start. Yet many people do this with viable relationships. Why?

Sometimes a relationship just needs to be tuned up and set back on track. Sometimes old patterns need to be changed; the parts of the engine have worn thin. Sometimes it requires an overhaul. Relationships are maintained in a healthy condition by two mechanics working full time.

Healthy relationships are special. They are holy: a child of God communicating to a child of God. Relationships need God's guidance. They cannot be maintained unaided. Turn to a higher power for guidance and strength. Admit powerlessness over human frailties. Find the ultimate ingredient for a healthy relationship.

If this all seems impossible, it is. But it is probable and certain if we have faith in a higher power who is leading us to love for one another.

Forgiveness

THE FUNCTION OF FORGIVENESS

Sexual addiction and coaddiction are indirectly connected to the search for the inner self, for the child of God within. These addictions are prompted by the misdirected longing to connect with God at a deep, spiritual level. In this search for meaning, people reach out for material substances. Addiction and coaddiction go hand in hand because they come out of the same place—a spiritual void.

Understanding this truth, individuals can address the addictive or codependent behaviors, forgive, and convert, moving to a new spiritual place.

It is not easy to let go of negative behaviors and find the way out of addiction and codependency. It is not easy to let go of love objects when one believes they fill our spiritual void. But in letting go to God, one finds the answers.

Forgiveness is the primary challenge of addicts and codependents, and the means whereby they find their way to peace of mind and recovery.

Why hold back? Some believe forgiveness is a gift to those who seem to have harmed us. It isn't. Forgiveness is always a gift to self. Holding back forgiveness simply means that the self has not been forgiven. Release of another person through forgiveness is the release of self.

Those who forgive are releasing themselves from illusions, while those who withhold forgiveness are binding themselves to illusions.

119

When I hold back forgiveness, I am into my own ego. Addiction and coaddiction are the same wrong. If you love too many too much, and I love you too much, what is the difference? Can there be a difference in degree of dysfunction? It seems both dysfunctional behaviors are really the same. Both partners are looking outside of self for worth; both are relying on external sources for validation.

Sexual addiction results from a need to be whole, an attempt to find connection and completion by getting high off another person. What is codependency but the same thing with fewer people? Both addictions limit personal power and stunt serious spiritual growth.

When the coaddicted person holds back forgiveness, that person chooses to deny or stay in the sickness. Releasing the other person is the beginning of freedom for the coaddict; it is the beginning of recovery.

It is impossible to talk about real forgiveness until the codependent has reached bottom, surrendered to the sickness, and experienced a spiritual awakening.

As Gerald Jampolsky writes in *Love Is Letting Go of Fear* (Berkeley, California: Celestial Arts, 1979, p. 24), "Forgiveness is the vehicle used for correcting our misconceptions and for helping us let go of fear. Simply stated, to forgive is to let go."

Letting go is surrender. In the final moments of surrender, the coaddict turns to God for the answers to the obsession. The coaddict understands the powerlessness and cannot do it alone. The object of obsession is as dangerous to the coaddict as alcohol is to an alcoholic. Powerless and in need of help, God becomes the only source of power to turn to. God becomes the solution.

God becomes the controlling force as the coaddict turns over his or her will and life to him. The addictive relationship is given to God. Thoughts of God replace the obsessive thoughts. The coaddict understands that no power but God can fill that spiritual void. The coaddict becomes God's child, filled with peace, love, and forgiveness. God is love; God is guiding the coaddict's life. God created all people out of love, and the primary function of all people is to forgive others.

At first it may take enormous concentration and courage to let go of obsessions, but this is the only way to freedom. Trying to control the addict and to manage the addiction only contributes to the disease. Letting this go to God helps everyone recover. It comes down to a simple cliché: "Mind your own business."

Your business is the business of God because you are God's child—you need to be about God's business. Using your gifts and developing your talents are his business and yours. Ask God for help and it will surely come to you.

Forgive yourself for having put another personal relationship above your relationship with God. Extend forgiveness to your loved one for having put other relationships before yours. There is no other way to the freedom of this new spiritual perspective, to the peace of mind all seek.

A NEW SPIRITUAL PERSPECTIVE

In a healthy relationship, you are connected with God first and with others through God. As a child of God, you are born of love itself. So is everyone else.

Each life is different because perspectives are different. When forgiveness becomes the primary function, there is no spiritual separation. All people are joined to a higher power. You become one with all and forgive others as you would be forgiven. In this primary relationship, you do not offer love to others but, with God, cocreate love.

Cocreating love is not an easy task. It is not love in the sense of popular songs. It is a divine union with another soul. It is the kind of love that joins two beings together. It is the kind of love that has no grievances.

So much in the world denies the possibility of unconditional love. But without it we know division, conflict, bargaining, and keeping score.

Gerald Jampolsky speaks of this bargaining as giving and getting:

We frequently have love/hate relationships in which we find ourselves trading conditional love. The getting motivation leads to conflict and distress, and is associated with linear time. Giving means extending one's love with no conditions, no expectations, and no boundaries. Peace of mind occurs, therefore, when we put all our attention into giving and have no desire to get anything from, or to change another person. The giving motivation leads to a sense of inner peace and joy that is unrelated to time. (*Love Is Letting Go of Fear*, p. 36)

Cocreating love begins within. Loving another comes out of the

121

experience with a loving God. It is God's love that all experience, and God's love that all pass on to others.

When cocreating love, we make no accusations. One's own "cry for love" is exactly the same as another's. Although the reflection in another of what one perceives as sin is repugnant, the cocreator acknowledges it within himself or herself, too. Unconditional love makes no accusations. We love others as God loves us.

Letting another go, allowing that person to be without judging, recognizing unacceptable behavior as a cry for love, is an acknowledgment that both of us are equal. In this oneness we know spiritual union.

Cocreation is an act performed in conjunction with love itself—God. The cocreator does not resist by grievances and revenge. In the simplest sense, God's love empowers cocreators to view themselves from a spiritual perspective—as children of God.

> *God is the Love in which I forgive myself,*
> *God is the Love with which I love myself,*
> *God is the Love in which I am blessed,*
> *No fear is possible in the mind beloved of God,*
> *God is the Love in which I forgive.*
> (*Course in Miracles*, Foundation for Inner Peace, P.O. Box 635, Tiburon, CA 94920.)

Having this new spiritual perspective, we learn to teach only love. This teaching includes no attacks or demands.

NO ATTACK THOUGHTS

It is difficult to remain vulnerable when betrayal is apparent. Attacking, however, does no more than aggravate the situation. Assuming a nondefensive posture, on the other hand, detaches the co-addict in a loving way from the addiction.

Detaching does not mean standing idly by and being abused. It simply means removing oneself emotionally—and physically, if necessary—from the attack. It never means mounting a counterattack.

Forgiveness involves loving actions that restrain the impulse to attack. Gaining a new spiritual perspective is not an incidental happening. It is not a simple switch in attitude. Rather, it is a profound, experiential occurrence which reaches the depths of our being. A sense of true forgiveness happens only after a transformation within. To want to forgive, to strive to forgive, to pretend to forgive won't work. Forgiveness has to come from within the center of the spiritual self. It has to come from the knowledge that God is a forgiving God whose children abide in this divine love. Seeing self in this light will help one to see others in the same light, the light of forgiveness.

Forgiveness is a profound metaphysical happening. To forgive and to be forgiven are primary functions in life. Without forgiveness, we cannot know peace. Accepting forgiveness from a loving God, then extending that forgiveness to others is not an easy task and may seem more like a small miracle. But when this miracle happens, freedom emerges. The need to attack or to make hidden demands ceases.

NO HIDDEN DEMANDS

Teach only love; do not make hidden demands. You might prefer to have your partner give the gift of fidelity, but you cannot demand it. Faithfulness achieved by a demand or ultimatum is coercion; faithfulness should be a free gift.

You can choose to leave a partner who is unfaithful, but you cannot serve an ultimatum that guarantees fidelity. The addict's recovery might be exacted through properly negotiated marriage contracts, but these pronouncements of fidelity must be offered freely. With the assistance of counseling and support groups, contracts may be set in place and guidelines established. Mutually negotiated contracts are not the same as unilateral demands.

You can make demands only on yourself. You can recover only from your own addiction. Hidden demands mask a cry for love and our own fear. Instead, teach only love, make no demands of God or of others.

If I am God's child,
I have all that I need
To be happy at this moment.
If I am God's child,
I am of love itself;
So I teach only love.

Codependent addiction to the addict comes from the same spir-

123

itual void from which the love addiction operates. Both addictions are spiritual sicknesses. The coaddict must get better by connecting with the true self, Love.

> *God is the Love in which I forgive myself,*
> *God is the Love with which I love myself,*
> *God is the Love in which I am blessed,*
> *No fear is possible in the mind beloved by God,*
> *God is the Love in which I forgive.*

RULES FOR FUNCTIONING WITH FORGIVENESS

Get rid of addictive demands. With a new spiritual perspective, it is possible to deal with addictive demands—the controlling ultimatums made to others, either subtly or aggressively, to satisfy personal needs for security, sex, or power. True, there are payoffs to demanding that a partner be faithful; e.g., protection from hurt, unhappiness, and public embarrassment. Also, it gives one power over the sex partner—ownership. However, this faithfulness seen as a right but purchased through addictive demands is unauthentic.

I remember one elaborate scheme I put together to get my husband to be faithful. On a carefully contrived romantic vacation, I convinced him to agree to a contract stating that he would avoid certain situations. That entire vacation was an addictive demand and could only lead to ultimate failure. Emotion-backed demands always lead to expectations which create unhappiness.

Learn to be happy. Someone once told me that God's will for me is happiness. I did not understand then, but I do now. Addictive demands for love always imply that the other person controls our personal happiness. Actually, the root of happiness lies in perception of self and relationship to one's self, others, and God. Only you can control your happiness. In order to be free and happy as God wills, one must give up addictive demands on self, on others, and finally, God.

The coaddict, connecting to another in an addictive way, generates his or her own unhappiness. The coaddict surrenders control of happiness.

Forgiveness is a gift to self. When you let go of others, you come back to yourself. You are the only person who can make you happy.

All expectations of happiness derived from those outside of self are doomed to disappointment and failure.

Change demands to preferences. Each of us harbors strong preferences. Preferences are much different from demands, however. A coaddict may prefer to be in a relationship with someone who is not sexually addicted to others. But the coaddict can't demand that the addict give up the addiction. The coaddict may prefer to discontinue living with someone who will not get treatment, or to separate from a person, place, or thing that triggers an emotion-packed addictive response.

The coaddict can forgive the addict's behavior, forgive his or her own behavior, forgive others involved, and make a decision to disconnect from that personal situation, moving on to a healthier place. Be warned, however, that taking a geographic cure from one sex addict sometimes only sets up the scene for a new relationship with another. If the coaddict does not get well, then the pattern repeats itself.

The coaddict may choose to stay in the relationship and work on recovery, allowing the spouse to work on recovery also.

Many options are open to the coaddict who understands that happiness is created. The coaddict can be happy in any situation if he or she is exercising *preference,* not demands.

Lovingly communicate by teaching only love. Forgiveness does not mean that one denies one's personal preferences for happiness. These preferences, however, must be carried out with loving communication. Otherwise, they may be misunderstood. Censure and condemnation have no place in a new spiritual perspective.

The partner with a spiritual perspective knows himself or herself as a child of God as deserving of forgiveness as the coaddict is. Loving communication, applied to all situations, becomes the directive to teach only love. When only love is taught, only love is received. The giving and receiving become one.

But you might say, how can I always be loving? What about anger, anxiety, jealousy, and fear? All these emotions are responses to addictive demands of others. Operating from the strength of preferences, however, one has no expectations for happiness outside of self. Therefore anger, anxiety, jealousy, and fear dissipate. If preferences are lovingly communicated but, in fact, are disguised demands, anger and revenge could result. Unhappiness will return. Preferences

125

are just that—preferences. They are not addictive demands.
Teach only love and it returns to you.

Reach for the inner self through prayer. To teach only love, one
must have a source of love available at all times. Here is where we
meet the child of God within. If we are of God, then we must be of
love too. It is there—within. One only needs to find it. Remember:

> *God is the love in which I forgive myself,*
> *God is the love with which I love myself,*
> *God is the love in which I am blessed,*
> *No fear is possible in the mind beloved of God,*
> *God is the love in which I forgive.*

Through prayer and meditation, you reach inside yourself to make
conscious contact with God. From that contact, you are empowered
to function with forgiveness, to preserve your own happiness, and to
teach love.

When scattered and pulled apart by the things of the world, a person can't be centered enough to deal with others. He or she won't be
able to think about self-image and responsibilities to self and others.

Prayers are reminders as well as affirmations. The world will pull
us off center if we allow it. We have so much to be concerned with.
What do you do to earn a living? Where will you live? With whom?
What is life all about? What are you here for?

Praying returns you to your inner being, to the child of God within. Praying returns you to the source of your power, to God, to love
itself. The structure of a life that functions in forgiveness is prayer.

Codependents think they can do everything. If they work hard
enough and long enough, the job will get done. But it never works.

In one who has a spiritual perspective, the management of life is
turned over to God. Through prayer, answers to difficult outside
problems are born within.

As Lynne Namka says in *The Doormat Syndrome,* "The process
of transformation includes the recognition and acknowledgment of
one's responsibility in contributing to a problem, despair over the
powerlessness of the situation and turning the situation over to a
Higher Power. The surrender is to the God Self.... Forgiveness at a
deep level is accomplished through humility and a longing to be free.
With release come gratitude and celebration. This is the rebirth as the

126

individual's belief systems are dramatically altered. Strength and integrity are felt as the integration of the personality is accomplished. A deep sense of humility and gratitude accompanies the surrender experience. Albert Camus described the death/rebirth experience when he said, 'In the midst of winter, I finally learned that there was in me an invincible summer.' " (Deerfield Beach, Florida: Health Communications, Inc., 1989, p. 143.)

You go to your own invincible summer when you reach inside yourself to pray. Consider these words from *The Course in Miracles:*

As I listen to God's voice, I am sustained by His Love. As I open my eyes, His Love lightens up the world for me to see. As I forgive, His Love reminds me that His Son is sinless. As I look upon the world with the vision he has given me, I remember that I am His [child]. (Tiburon California: Foundation for Inner Peace, 1985, p. 100.)

These words remind us that to be serene, we have to draw from within. We have to reach the child of God within to hear God's voice. It is very simple. Find a quiet spot to get connected with God and pray. Then listen.

By turning problems over to God, we find solutions. Vulnerability becomes our greatest strength because it allows God to work through us. By teaching only love and practicing forgiveness, we become tools that God can work with. We can be the living examples of his love. We can exemplify reconciliation, redemption, or salvation.

Recognize reconciliation already accomplished. If we are all children of God, we are of love itself. If we are of love itself, then we are already reconciled with all other beings around us. Human forgiveness seems to be an outward sign of something that has already occurred within.

> *The reconciliation*
> *between you and me*
> *has already taken place*
> *in the mind*
> *and heart of God.*
> *So, it is just a matter of time*
> *until we catch up,*

*whether it be in this world
or the next.*

If God is love, resentment and anger make no sense at all. They exist only in our minds. Reconciliation has occurred already if we are of God; we might as well extend it through human forgiveness.

It would be difficult to think of a loving God as condemning the sex addict and forgiving the coaddict. Both have loved too much. God forgives both. In God's mind, reconciliation has already taken place. We only need to implement it.

Letting go of guilt, fear, anxiety, judgment, hypervigilance, compulsive behavior, denial, and other negative behaviors is difficult. The only way is by asking God for help. Surrender to a loving God, accept his forgiveness for self as well as for others. In surrendering, we find peace; we are free.

To withhold forgiveness is to be less than what we really are—children of God. When we hold back, we reject freedom. Perhaps we are still afraid or wish to hang on to the addict or are unable to connect with a higher power. Perhaps we have not established a clear picture of ourselves as a child of God, filled with love and joined to our brothers and sisters. Perhaps we do not believe that God's plan is for love, not separation.

Forgiveness is the starting place, the only place.

*God is the Love in which I forgive myself,
God is the Love with which I love myself,
God is the Love in which I am blessed,
No fear is possible in the mind beloved of God,
God is the Love in which I forgive.*

CHAPTER

TEN

The Primary Relationship

Filling a spiritual void within by relying on an outside force is what codependency is all about. The fear of abandonment drives the coaddict to cling to another person with an addictive tenacity. The feeling of separateness makes the coaddict so terrified. However, what can fill that spiritual void?

THE PRIMARY RELATIONSHIP: SELF AND GOD

To the question of filling the void within, there is only one answer: love, union with God. Without a sense of connection to a higher power, the coaddict will be left feeling empty and alone.

Recently, I heard a member of a twelve-step group say that he felt as if he had been born with a "divine disquietude" that could only be filled through his relationship with God. For him, nothing else could fill the emptiness inside.

It is the inability to deal with aloneness creatively that drives people to a codependent state; it is this aloneness that enables a coaddict to contribute to another's addiction.

When anyone values a relationship so much that it directs one's life, that person has given God-like power to the other person or to that relationship.

Making a human relationship primary and neglecting the most primary relationship—God and self—causes people to lose the way.

Spiritual intimacy with a higher power transcends human relationships. Addiction and coaddiction involve forgetting God or, at best, putting the relationship with God in second place.

How do you get back on track?

The first way is to recognize that you are off track. By reading this book, you are reaching out to find the answer to a dependency that has caused you spiritual harm. By trying to evaluate what is wrong in your life, you are defining the problem and progressing toward a solution, a new spirituality. By accepting the premise that life is more than what you have known, you are part way to this new life.

In all relationships, a certain amount of energy must be expended in order to be successful. So it is with God and self. To reap the benefits of this divine relationship, you need to make conscious contact with God. That means prayer and meditation.

When anything is important to you, you devote yourself to it. Your primary relationship with God is the most essential thing in life. Yet, if you do not tend to it, you will not become aware of the benefits of such a union. The inner spiritual void will remain.

People often say they need time to work around the house, to relax, to play, to be with friends or even to attend church events. But how often do people say they are going to meditate? A spiritual relationship with God is personal and may require a reflective, quiet tone at times. Nevertheless, conscious contact can be made with God in any setting: in the car, at work, or before sleep.

When I realized that I was anxious to be in contact with God, I knew I had moved to a different level of prayer. No longer was it a "duty" to pray, but a much sought after and welcome activity. I found that it refueled and empowered me for the other relationships of my life. My prayer became a jealously guarded time I needed to exist.

Like a child, I began to turn to my parent, God, and hand over control of my life. God controlled and guided all my important human relationships. My prayerful connection with God became the most important relationship. Without this commitment, I seemed to lose my way, forgetting that I am loved, protected, and cared for at all times.

SEEING MYSELF AS A CHILD OF GOD

It was only when I began to see myself as a child of God that I began to view others in the same way. When I came to this realization, my relationships with others changed. Forgiveness became easier because I felt I was one with others in love of God. We are all his children.

It became clearer to me that even though I might not find someone else's behavior acceptable, I did not have to judge. My primary functions became forgiveness, understanding, and tolerance. Even if it became necessary for me to step out of the way of someone else's negative actions, I still did not have to alter my view of them as a child of God. Wonderful things started to happen!

Forgiveness, understanding, and tolerance heal. Anger, resentment, and intolerance generate pain. Where there was discord in my life, I found no peace. When I got on track with my most primary relationship—myself and God—all other relationships began to shift in their perspective.

It would be hard to imagine that God condemns differences in people. Why, then, should I? There are differences in people's behavior, but it is no longer my job to understand them. I do not have God's insight into the condition of any human soul, nor do I wish to. All I know is that today a loving God is nurturing and caring for my spiritual self. That may be all I need to know.

The codependent can spend a lifetime looking to others to find happiness and never find it. When the codependent looks within and gets connected to a higher power or God, he or she finds that happiness. If this sounds simple, it is!

MAKING CONSCIOUS CONTACT WITH GOD

Reaching within helps us to make conscious contact with the higher power. It means directing the mind to that loving place of comfort, thinking of and speaking to God. When we make conscious contact with God, God's presence becomes evident in all living things. We gain possession of a living spirituality.

The many distractions in the material world make it easy to lose contact with God. In order to stay connected, we must reach out through prayer, reading, and meditation.

In *Spirituality and Recovery*, Father Leo Booth describes meditation as "a technique of realizing our full potential as human beings and living our lives to the fullest. It is about finding time and discovering the time 'to be.' It is placing the physical, mental, and emotional aspects of our lives in an 'at one-ment.' It is using silence to say 'yes'." (*Spirituality and Recovery,* Deerfield Beach, Florida:

131

Health Communications, 1985, p. 84).

Meditation has no set pattern; it is primarily experiential. It is being still and knowing God. It is being still and being grateful to God. It is concentrating on the word *peace* or *love* until it is internalized. It may be reading special words meditatively. It is different for each person but for all it awakens the spark of the divine within us.

By paying too much attention to relationships, career, or even the care and management of a home, we can lose our spiritual center and forget to contact God. When this happens, we are looking for happiness outside ourselves—in things, in people. That never works. Joy begins within.

Conscious contact with others can bring special moments of spiritual connection, holy "instants." When we give of ourselves, we receive. But first we have to have our own spirit charged. It takes emotional energy to give of self. When there is little inside, we are soon depleted. Making contact with God keeps us empowered; it keeps us in the right place. It fills in the spiritual void so that we may give to others.

When I become overwhelmed with the ups and downs of life, I feel powerless. However, when I am in the right place with God, I find enough power to deal not only with the obstacles of life, but also to overcome them. God, the creator of all love, gives me enough love to live, to forgive, to accept, and to grow.

GOD'S WILL FOR ME IS JOY

It seems inconceivable that God's will for me is anything but joy.

So much of what we see in our everyday living is seen from the wrong perspective. We see material loss, death, and suffering. Expecting to understand all these things can become overwhelming. It is so much simpler to accept God's will for me as joy and to leave the rest to God.

I do not know why life includes so many shifts and changes. How often I cope with it, however, through illusion—the illusion that I can make sense of it and control it—when in reality it works out without me.

By recognizing that my primary relationship is with God, I can let go of the things of this world and not expect to understand them. I can let go of an addictive relationship knowing that it was not meant to bring me joy. Loss always includes sadness, but the sadness is easier to bear when I do not resist the change, when I "let go and let God."

By really believing that God's will for me is joy, I can view loss as normal and look for the good that inevitably will come from it. As a codependent person, I tended toward a rigidity that defied change. I was unable to let go even when I understood that it was necessary. By letting go to God and believing that the outcome of all events will be joy, I discovered hope, and now living makes sense.

As long as I played God, trying to control the world, I did not find joy. When I let go and brought my will in line with God's, I found joy.

SPECIAL RELATIONSHIPS AND HOLY INSTANTS

We are spiritual creatures who can determine our own destiny through decision, action, and belief. Yet we sometimes do not choose to live spiritually. We prefer aloneness to the risks of relationship.

Fear immobilizes, pushing us toward loneliness. Fear is the symptom of addiction and codependency. Although a relationship with God is the key to the discovery of a spiritual life, God is also manifested in the world, in people. It is through relationships that we continue to discover our own energy, our own spirituality, and God.

Because God works through people, we need to be open to those holy instants that make up our existence, to those soul-sharing moments that help to keep us in touch with the child of God within us and others.

It is difficult to think of a spiritual life without the combination of self, others, and God. Prioritizing these relationships is somewhat futile since they seem to work together in an interdependent as well as independent way.

In *Spirituality and Recovery,* Father Leo Booth points out that "only when we feel good about ourselves and good about our relationship with others, will we be able to understand what it means to be a child of God. The energizing joy of self-love creates healthy relationships with others. Therefore, in our pursuit of the spiritual life, we need to consider relationships" (p. 93).

For the coaddict who reads this book, recovery comes when you break loose to discover this miracle within, when you accept yourself and others as children of God by looking within, not outside of self. From that moment of recognition of your own addictive behavior comes the corrective balance in your relationship to self, to others, and to God.

This book ends in a loving place with the wish that all of us, as children of God, might see each other as equals in God's love. None of us is without human frailty, yet we are all perfect just as we are. We are all holy in God's love; we are free, free from the addictive cycle of sexual addiction and coaddiction, free from the tyranny of its symptoms—denial, obsession, and compulsive behavior.

At a spiritual level, we can put the physical behaviors aside for the moment as we commemorate our oneness in God's love. We can celebrate all relationships as special, we can regret no part of a journey that brought us closer to our true self, others, and God. We can deem this moment our holy instant.

Sources of Help

Suggested Reading

Out of the Shadows: Understanding Sexual Addiction, by Patrick Carnes, Ph.D., 1983.
Currently published by Hazelden Educational Materials, PO Box 176, Center City, MN
55012-0176.

Contrary to Love: Helping the Sexual Addict, by Patrick Carnes, Ph.D., 1989.
Currently published by Hazelden.

A Gentle Path Through the Twelve Steps, by Patrick Carnes, Ph.D., 1992.
Published by Hazelden.

Don't Call It Love: Recovery from Sexual Addiction, by Patrick Carnes, Ph.D., 1991.
Published by Bantam Books, 666 Fifth Ave., New York, NY 10103.

Lonely All the Time: Recognizing, Understanding and Overcoming Sex Addiction, for Addicts and Codependents, by Ralph Earle, Ph.D. and G. Crow, 1989. Psychological Counseling Services, 7530 E. Angus Dr., Scottsdale, AZ 82521

Hope and Recovery: A Twelve-Step Guide for Healing From Compulsive Sexual Behavior. 1987.
Currently published by Hazelden.

Women, Sex, and Addiction: A Search for Love and Power, by Charlotte Davis Kasl, Ph.D., 1989.
Published by Ticknor & Fields, 52 Vanderbilt Avenue, New York, NY 10017.

Faithful & True: Healing the Wounds of Sexual Addiction, by Mark Lauser, Ph.D., 1992.
Published by Zondervan Publishers, Inc., Grand Rapids, MI 49530.

Is It Love or is it Addiction? by Brenda Schaeffer, 1987.
Currently published by Hazelden Educational Materials, Center City, MN.

Back From Betrayal: Recovering From his Affairs, by Jennifer P. Schneider, M.D., Ph.D.
1988. Published by Ballantine Books, 201 E. 50 St., New York, NY 10022.

Sex, Lies, and Forgiveness: Couples Speak on Healing From Sex Addiction, by J. Schneider and B. Schneider, 1991and 1999.
Published by Recovery Resources Press, 7272 E. Broadway, PMB 372, Tucson, AZ 85710.

Women Who Love Sex Addicts; Help for Healing from the Effects of a Relationship with a Sex Addict, by Douglas Weiss and Diane DeBuske, 1993. Published by Discovery Press, 6500 West Freeway, Suite 202, Fort Worth, TX 76116.

The Final Freedom: Pioneering Sexual Addiction Recovery by Douglas Weiss, Ph.D., 1998. Published by Discovery Press, 6500 West Freeway, Suite 202, Fort Worth, TX 76116.

For the Addict:

Support Groups

Sexaholics Anonymous (SA)
PO Box 111910
Nashville, TN 37222-1910
(615) 331-6230
http://www.sa.org

Sex & Love Addicts Anonymous (SLAA)
P.O. Box 338
Norwood, MA 02062-0338
(781) 255-8825
http://www.slaafws.org
fwsoffice@slaafws.com

Sex Addicts Anonymous (SAA)
PO Box 70949
Houston, TX 77270
(713) 869-4902
1-800-447-8191
http://www.sexaa.org
info@saa-recovery.org

Sexual Compulsives Anonymous (SCA)
Old Chelsea Station, PO Box 1585
New York, NY 10013-0935
(212) 439-1123 or 800-977-HEAL
http:// www.sca-recovery.org

Sexual Recovery Anonymous (SRA)
PO Box 73, Planetarium Station
New York, NY 10024
(212) 340-4650

Sexual Assault Recovery Anonymous:
PO Box 72044
Burnaby, BC V5H 4PQ Canada
(606) 290-9382

For the Partner or Family Member:

Codependents of Sex Addicts (COSA)
9337-B Katy Freeway, Suite 142
Houston, TX 77024
(612) 537-6904
http://www.shore.net/~cosa

S-Anon International Family Groups
PO Box 111242
Nashville, TN 37222-1242
(615) 833-3152

Recovering Couples Anonymous (RCA)
PO Box 11872
St. Louis, MO 63105
(314) 830-2600

For Sexual Trauma Survivors:

Survivors of Incest Anonymous (SIA)
PO Box 21817
Baltimore, MD 21222
(410) 282-3400

Incest Survivors Anonymous (ISA)
PO Box 17245
Long Beach, CA 90807
(562) 428-5599

Sexual Assault Recovery Anon. (SARA)
PO Box 16
Surrey, BC, V35 424 Canada

Printed in the United States
22956LVS00001B/152